award winning architectural studio

formafatal

award-winning architectural studio

TCA Think Tank Editions

formafatal

colophon

formafatal
award winning architectural studio

formafatal, s.r.o.

Jaromírova 431/29
128 00Praha 2
Czech Republic

formafatal@formafatal.cz
www.formafatal.cz

author
formafatal

editor
Pier Alessio Rizzardi

© TCA Think Tank Editions.
All rights are reserved.
No parts of this publication may be reproduced, stored in a retrieval system or transmitted, in any form or by any means, electronic, mechanical, photocopying, recording or otherwise, without the prior permission of TCA Editions.

Every effort has been made to gain permission from copyright holders and/or Photographer, where known, for images reproduced in this book, and care has been taken to caption and credit those images correctly.

Any omission are unintentional and we will be happy to include appropriate credit in future editions if further information is brought to the publisher's attention.

TCA Think Tank Editions
Books on Architecture

First published in September 2022 by
TCA Think Tank Editions
Powered by TCA Think Tank Pte. Ltd.

Singapore: 20 Depot ln, 109763, Singapore
Italy: Research Center, Via Bettinelli, 4, 20136 Milan

www.tcathinktankeditions.com

ISBN 978-1-9164537-8-4

award winning architectural studio

Contents

Who We Are	6
What We Do	7
Residential- Costa Rica	**8**
Art Villa	10
Atelier Villa	34
Coco Villa	62
Residential - Czech Republic	**85**
Hřebejkovi	86
Slezská	96
Loft Hřebenky	106
Strom Flat	120
Residential - Sri Lanka	**134**
Happy Hills	136
Hospitality - Czech Republic	**151**
Moon Club	152
Gran Fierro II	174
Gran Fierro I	196
Autentista	208
Burrito Loco	220

who we are

We're a team of friends - architects, designers, and set designers.
We're a creative studio focused on architecture, interior design, exhibition installation, and product design.
Formafatal studio became the winner of the category Emerging Interior Designer Of The Year - DEZEEN AWARDS 2020.

The studio was founded by architect Dagmar Štěpánová and she leads and owns the studio together with Katarína and Jan. The team is now Dagmar, Katarína, Jan, Iveta, Dana, Anna, Debora, Petra and Lucie.

what we do

A team of nine professionals is currently working on several commercial and residential projects in the Czech Republic and across the world. Formafatal studio has already won several international and domestic awards for its completed interior projects. "We create public spaces, where people feel cozy, and homes, that are tailored to the clients' needs. All projects we approach individually and with a focus on specific human needs and clients' requirements. The individual approach for each project is based on mutual understanding with the client, enthusiasm, natural collaboration, and unified conceptual solutions. We solve projects complexly from creative concept to realization, with attention to detail. To us, our work means life and passion. In our projects, we often cooperate with other artists because we love to support talented individuals—together with them, we create original and innovative spaces that cultivate society. The emphasis on sustainability is a matter of course in our projects. In our approach to architecture, we also consider and accentuate historical values that we always try to preserve."

residential

award-winning architectural studio

costa rica

award-winning architectural studio

art villa
family house for holiday rental

Architect in Charge
Eng. Arch Dagmar Štěpánová (Formafatal)
Eng. Arch Jan Skoupý (Refuel works)

Team authors - architects
Eng. Arch Dagmar Štěpánová (Formafatal)
Eng. Arch Martina Homolková (Formafatal)
Eng. Arch Jan Skoupý (Refuel works)
Eng. Arch Zbyněk Ryška (Refuel works)

Location
Bahia Ballena, Costa Rica

Area
Built-up area 618 m^2
usable floor area 570 m^2

Project Year
2016-2018

Realization completed
2020

Photo credit:
BoysPlayNice (www.boysplaynice.com)

Awards & Nominations
Dezeen Awards 2020 - Shortlisted "House Interior Category"
A+AWARDS Architizer - The Project Of The Month (May 2020)

formafatal

residential

residential

Nested on the jungle hill, overlooking the rich coast of the Pacific ocean, 300m (1000 feet) above the ocean, 1km up the unpaved road so steep that 4x4 off-road car can hardly make it, there you find a distinctive complex of Art villas, three unique constructions created to enjoy, relax and reconnect with nature.

The two-story villa holds a prominent spot on the premises of 25 000 m², with a floor area of 570 m². Apart from the generous common area, the villa is equipped with five bedrooms with private bathrooms. In the basement, there is a playroom, a gym, a dance hall, a walk-in closet, a laundry room, and utility rooms.

The idea was to create a place where everyone can connect with the surrounding nature, clear their mind, and relax, enjoying the exceptional view, where everybody can experience both luxury and adventure, becoming a place that gets deep into your heart.

Inspired not only in the surrounding wild jungle but also in the work of the Brazilian architect Paulo Mendez da Rocha we intentionally left the concrete walls raw, complementing the interior components, selected materials, water, and greenery altogether, creating a unique environment, both rough and luxurious.

Monolithic concrete construction was a challenging vision. Nevertheless, we wanted to build a solid house that proudly stood naked in the raw lush vegetation. House that will last for many years. Modern yet timeless. Minimalistic but opulent. Tropical but robust. Jungle-wood features, expansive glass walls, and brave dimensions ignite, absorb, and reflect the raw elements of nature. Glide across floors paved in handmade Nicaraguan tiles.

The ever-changing patterns and colors are a reflection of the elusive and unique nature. The hand-painted watercolor jungle motif on the kitchen backsplash is another interior highlight, serving as a mirror reflecting life behind the wall; the wall becomes a window allowing us to see the nature outside.

Art Villa is mainly furnished with furniture designed by the studio and custom-made by local artisans or manufactured in the Czech Republic and then brought to the site.

Teak wood, metal, and concrete – these materials dominate the villa interiors. With custom-made furniture pieces in secondary pastel and bright colors, the raw concrete monolithic interior truly becomes alive with a touch of softness.

award-winning architectural studio

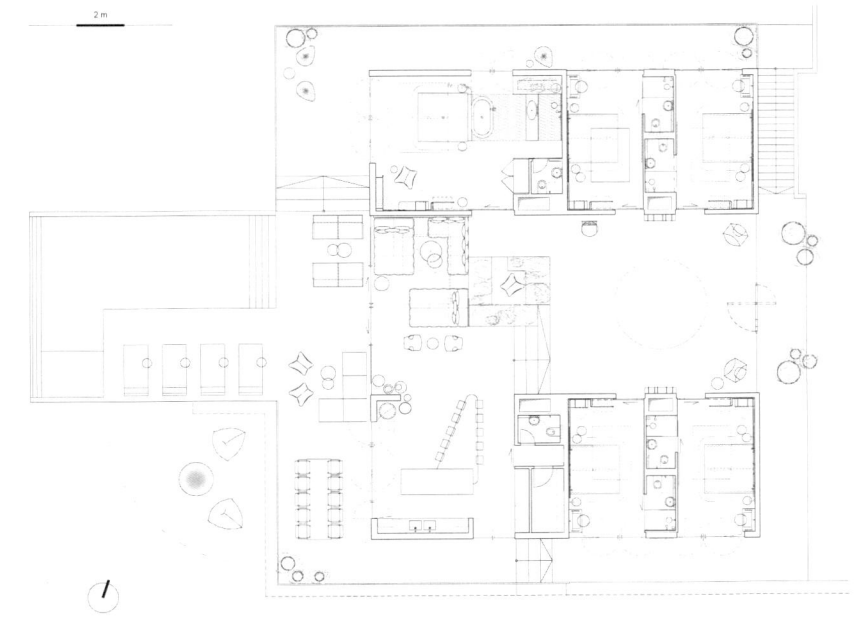

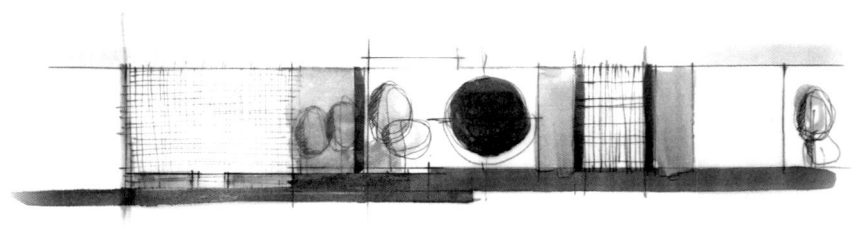

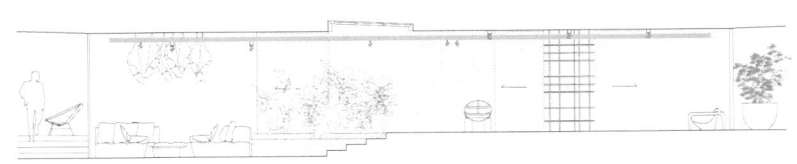

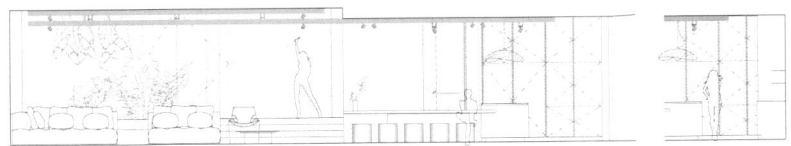

art villa

award-winning architectural studio

award-winning architectural studio

art villa

residential

award-winning architectural studio

art villa

award-winning architectural studio

art villa

residential

award-winning architectural studio

art villa

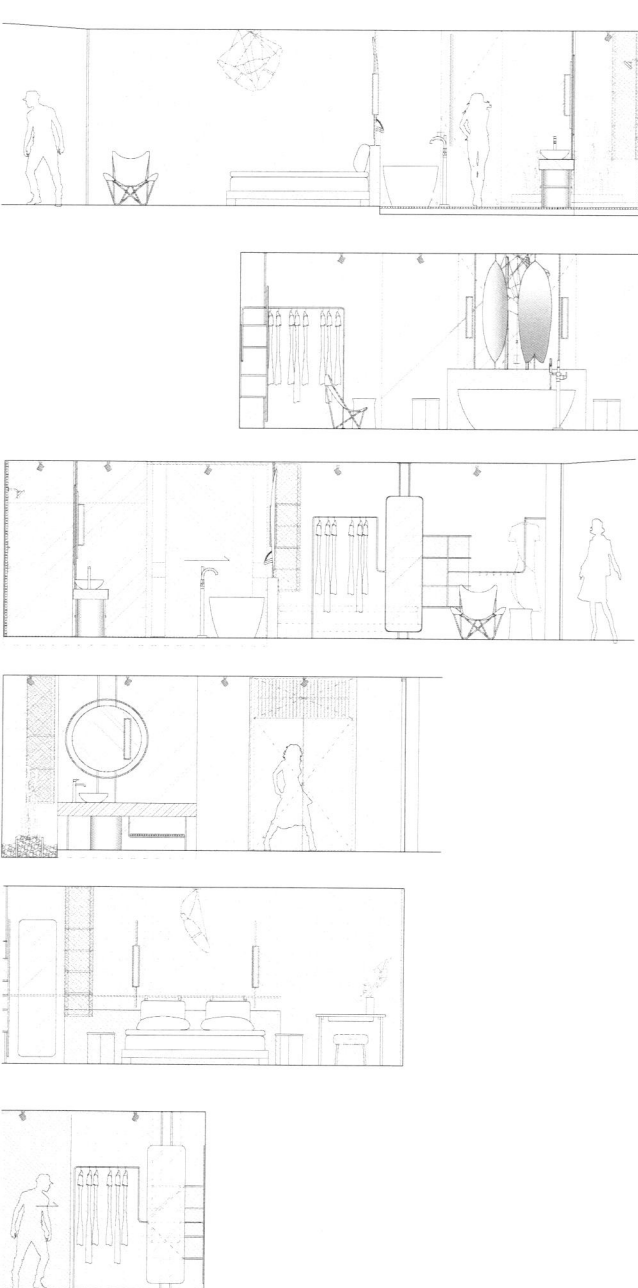

award-winning architectural studio

art villa

award-winning architectural studio

art villa

award-winning architectural studio

art villa

award-winning architectural studio

atelier villa
family house for holiday rental

Architect in Charge
Eng. Arch Dagmar Štěpánová

Team authors - architects
Eng. Arch Dagmar Štěpánová
Eng. Arch Martina Homolková

Location
Bahia Ballena, Costa Rica

Area
Built-up area 326 m^2
Usable floor area 298 m^2

Project Year
2017-2018

Realization completed
2020

Photo credit
BoysPlayNice (www.boysplaynice.com)

Awards & Nominations
A+AWARDS 2020 Architizer - WINNER "Residential PrivateE House category (3000-5000 sqft)
Dezeen Awards 2020 - Longlisted "Rural House category"
Interior Of The Year 2020 Czech Republic - Finalist "Private Interior (New Building) category

residential

Atelier villa is a second house from three unique constructions created to live in and rent. As the first villa is the solid concrete house, the Atelier villa is "light", modern, cost-effective idea for a tropical home. It is protected yet completely open, standing out and blending in at the same time. Distinctive but at the same time fitting in the place. Simple yet playful.

We built a home nestled in nature, spacious and unbound by convention. Thanks to the clever construction thought to every detail; you feel connected with the surrounding nature. You can experience the freedom of the imagining mind merging with the organic world. There are no set boundaries between inside and outside. The place becomes a space where one can reach out and meet nature and get lost in stars, which you can see through a unique facade.

The main inspiration was the place itself, surrounding nature, and the idea to create a place where you feel like being part of the whole—the idea of erasing boundaries between interior and exterior highlighting constructional simplicity and pure lines. Designed carefully and with maximum respect for nature. The biggest challenge when designing the house was the green roof, adding $1{,}5 t/m^2$ in a seismic most active area with only one bearing/outside wall and with a limited budget.

The green roof is not only merging with the surrounding landscape but there is no need to use A/C in the house, thanks to this idea.

Nestled against a steep slope, the 26-meter-long prismatic object partially levitates over lush tropical vegetation. Although the house's layout is very open, lightweight sliding partition walls may serve to create private zones and transform the space as needed.

The patio reveals an infinity pool, partly roofed therefore protected from the scorching sun.
The ocean and jungle-oriented lifting facades are fitted with large-size aluminum perforated sections that are rust-resistant and do not heat up in the sun. The full-back wall is in charred timber cladding treated with Shou Sugi Ban technique, an old Japanese weather-resistant wood treatment technique. Most of the furnishings are tailor-designed for this villa and custom-made.

award-winning architectural studio

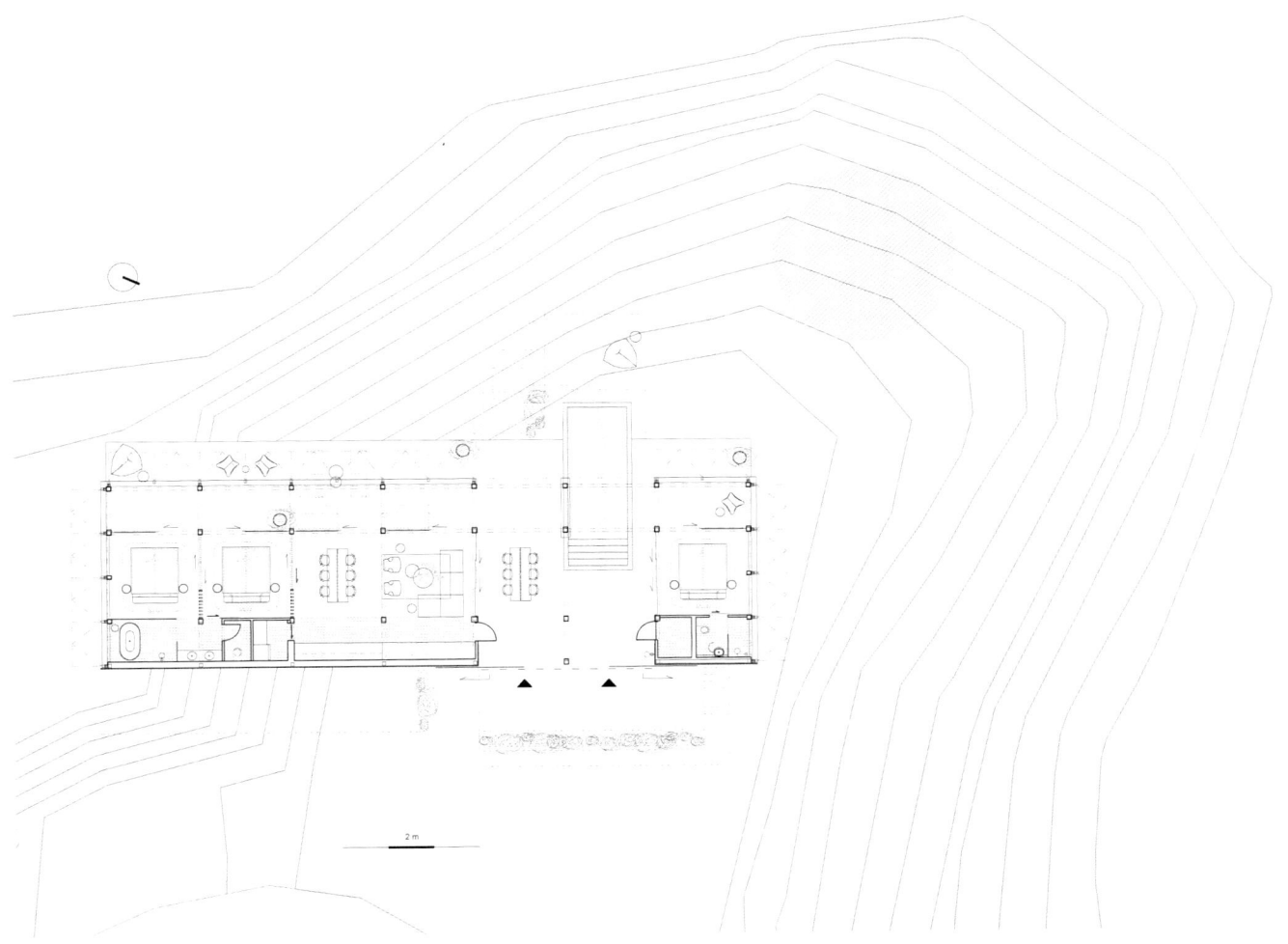

atelier villa

award-winning architectural studio

atelier villa

award-winning architectural studio

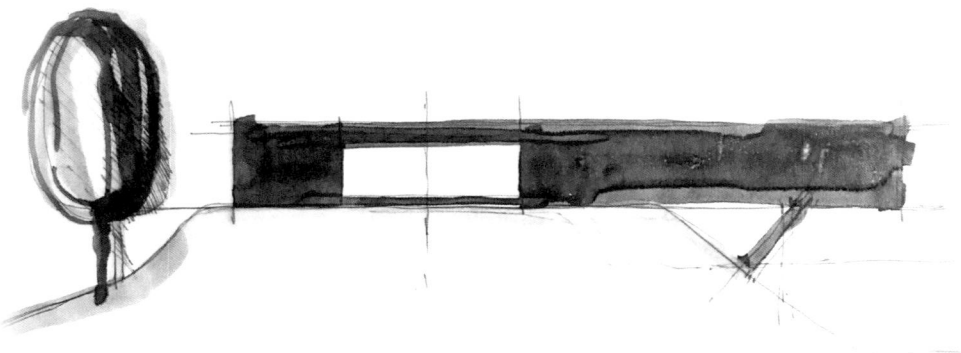

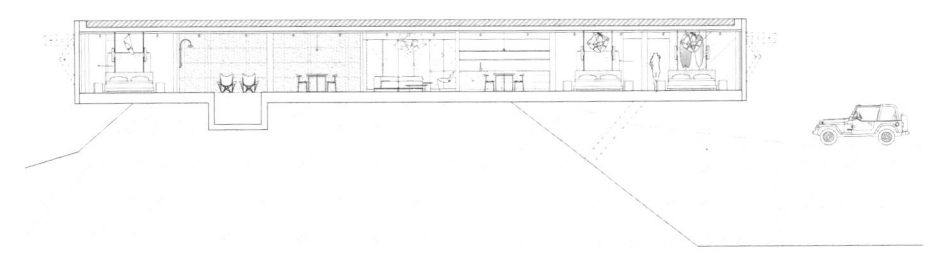

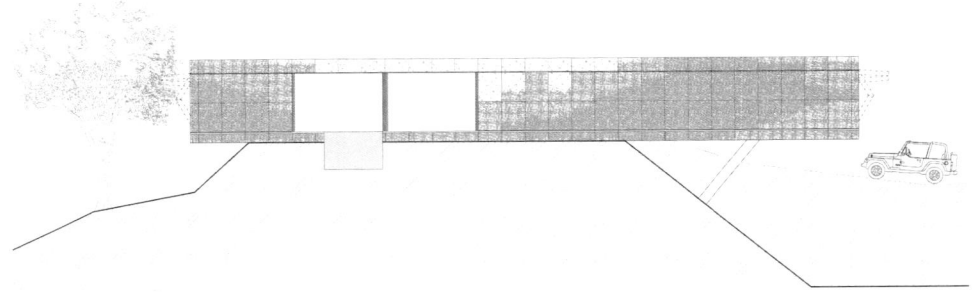

atelier villa

residential

formafatal

award-winning architectural studio

atelier villa

award-winning architectural studio

atelier villa

49

residential

formafatal

award-winning architectural studio

atelier villa

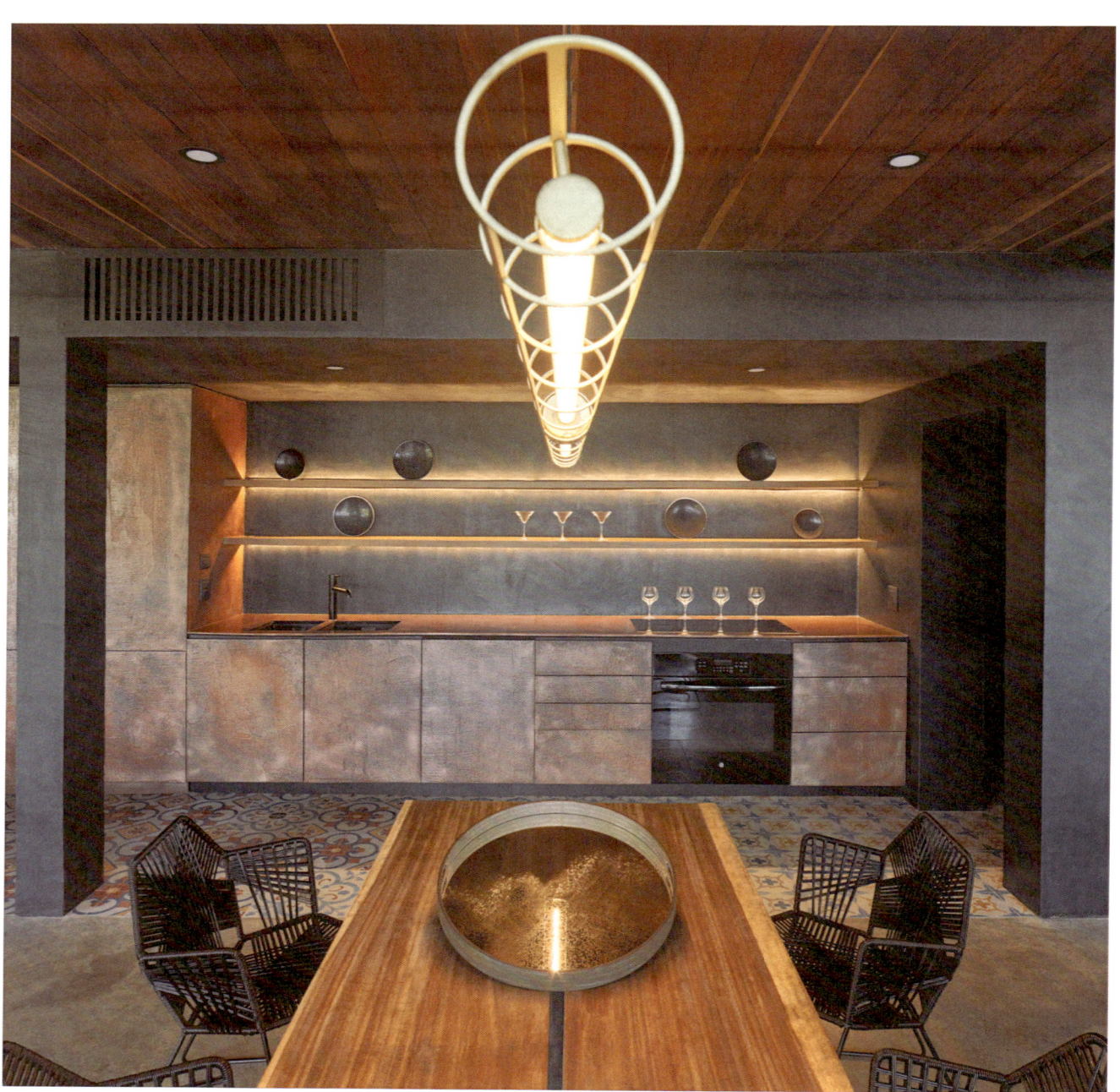

award-winning architectural studio

atelier villa

formafatal

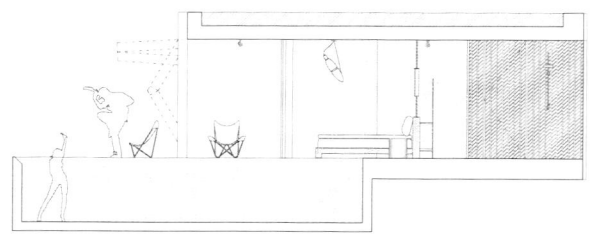

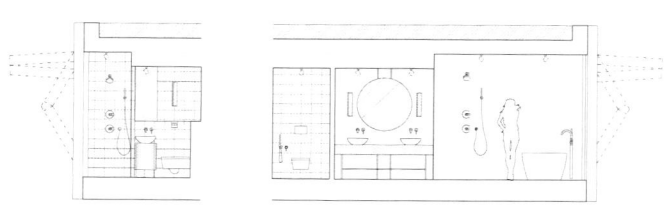

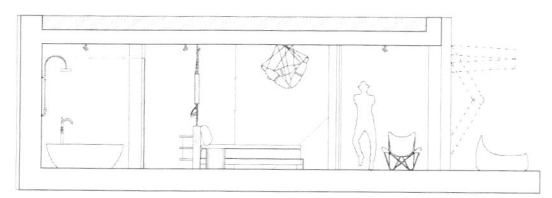

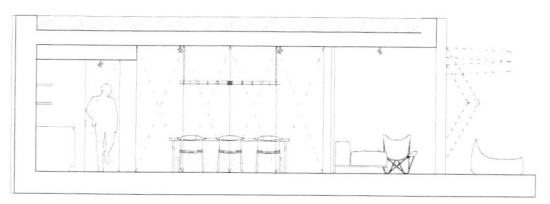

award-winning architectural studio

atelier villa

award-winning architectural studio

atelier villa

residential

formafatal

award-winning architectural studio

atelier villa

award-winning architectural studio

coco villa
cabins for holiday rentals

Architect in Charge
Eng. Arch Dagmar Štěpánová (Formafatal)
Eng. Arch Martin Kloda (Archwerk)

Team authors - architects
Eng. Arch Dagmar Štěpánová (Formafatal)
Eng. Arch Martin Kloda (Archwerk)
Eng. Arch Hana Procházková (Archwerk)

Location
Bahía Ballena, Puntarenas, Costa Rica

Area
Usable floor interior area 140 m²
Terraces 204 m²

Project Year
2018 - 2019

Photo credit
BoysPlayNice (www.boysplaynice.com)

Realization completed
2020

residential

CoCo houses are inspired by seed cones, where nature contains its precious promise to the future—designed to relax in comfortable, charming spaces. Luxuriate place high above ground level with a view to a brilliant expanse of green life. It is an effort to bring nature into life as much as possible and make it another family member.

The Coco complex prides itself in the lightness and grace of its construction solution, and we did not want to lose any of it when designing the layout of Coco interiors. That is why we have decided only to use the bare minimum of partition walls as high as 2.1m to separate different zones – bedroom, bathroom, closet. The bed is draped in a mosquito net, thus creating the core of the Coco cabin. The core and its shell, so similar in shape, both the small within the large and the large within the small. There are wooden floors in two levels in all Coco houses, only for the bathrooms; we used handmade cement tiles with a pattern from Nicaragua.

Each of the four CoCo houses has one bedroom with an ensuite bathroom and closet. In addition, there is one CoCo house with living space, Kitchen, Terrace, Pool & Toboggan. Individual Cocos are interconnected via walkways and terraces floating high above the ground, just like the cabins themselves. The walkway network over the ground allows the inhabitants of all cabins to walk directly to the central Coco house, which serves as a common area with a kitchen and dining room.

When it comes to interior design, the headboards are distinctive elements. Welded wire mesh sheet interwoven with various cords and ropes reminds us that Coco lies high above the ground, in the canopy of trees, where cords and ropes serve their purpose. Each Coco cabin is fitted with a different combination of these to create different vibes. Here you may find cement floors, but only in the bathrooms and in relatively subtle colors and patterns compared to other villas. All Coco bedrooms are identical in the interior, differing in artistically designed headboards made of braided curry nets. The idea to use ropes and straps arose from the exact location of small buildings high above the ground (Canopy).

award-winning architectural studio

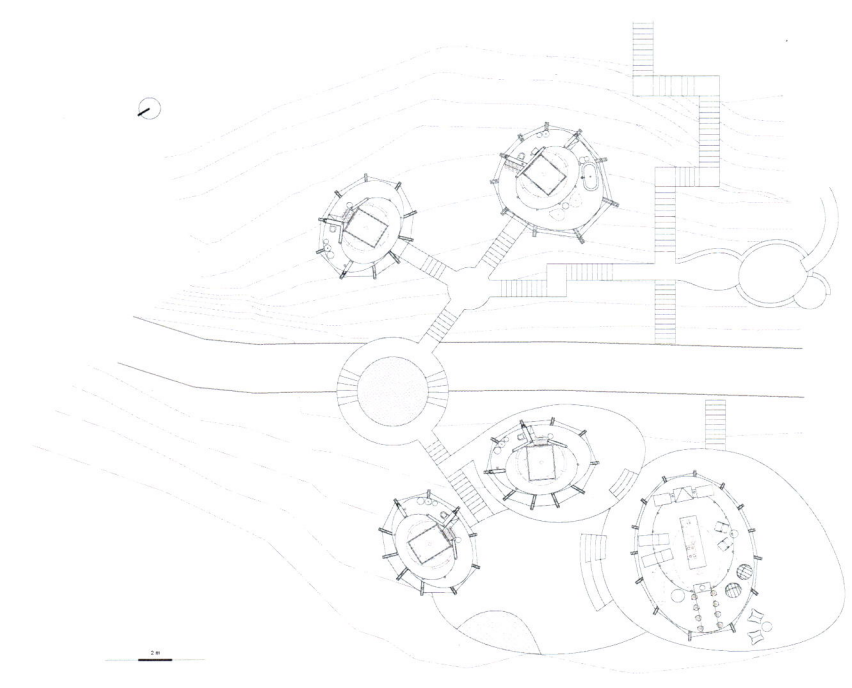

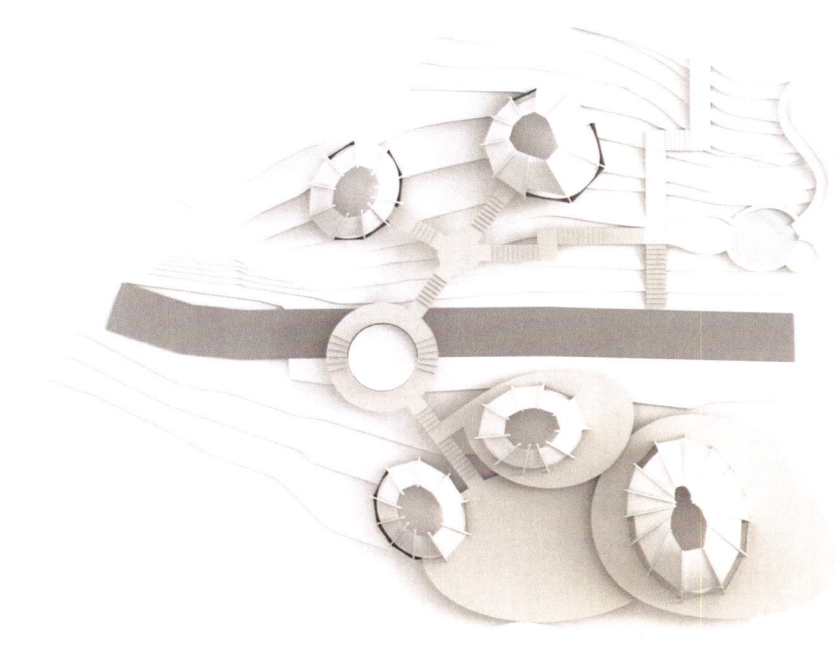

coco villa

award-winning architectural studio

coco villa

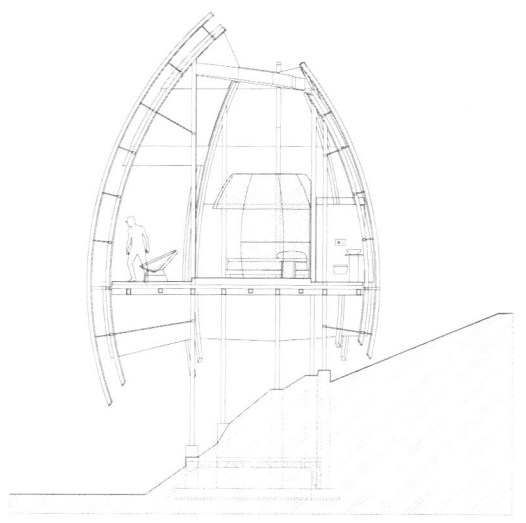
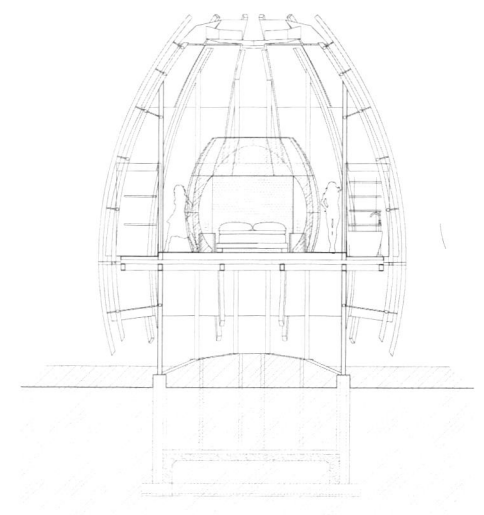
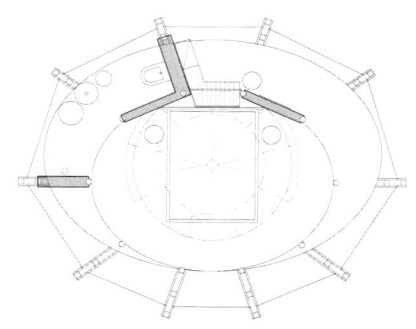
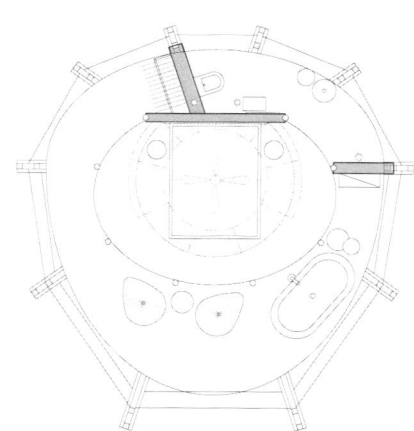

2 m

award-winning architectural studio

coco villa

award-winning architectural studio

coco villa

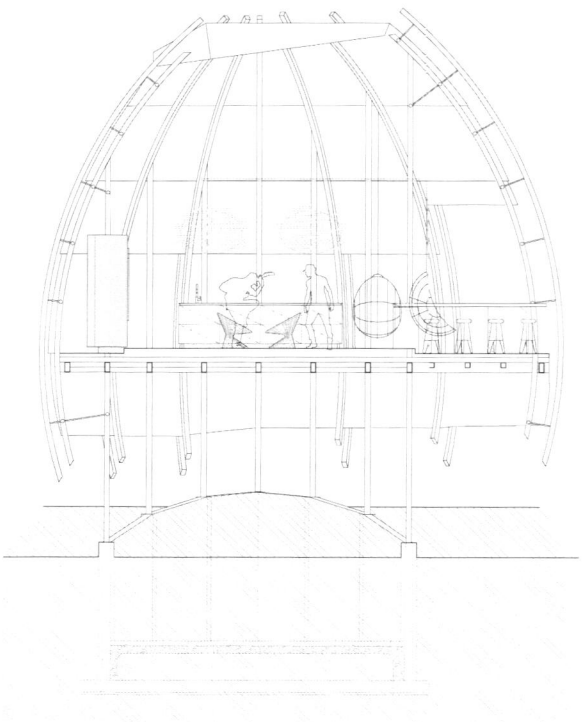
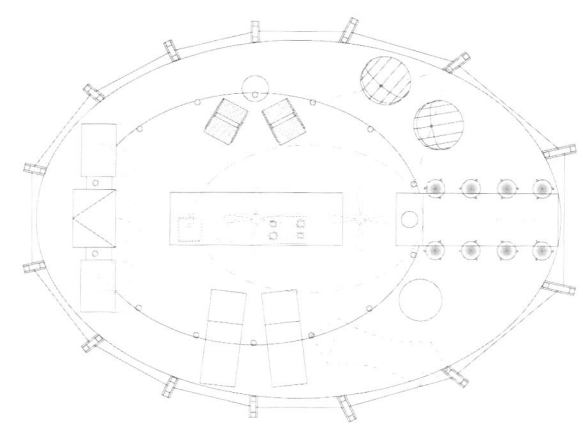

2 m

award-winning architectural studio

coco villa

award-winning architectural studio

coco villa

award-winning architectural studio

coco villa

residential

award-winning architectural studio

czech republic

award-winning architectural studio

hřebejkovi
family house

Architect in Charge
Eng. Arch Dagmar Štěpánová

Team authors - architects
Eng. Arch Dagmar Štěpánová

Location
Prague, Czech Republic

Area
Usable floor interior area 100 m²
Terraces 75 m²

Project Year
2016-2018

Realization completed
2020

Photo credit
BoysPlayNice (www.boysplaynice.com)

Awards & Nominations
Interior Of The Year 2020 Czech Republic - Finalist "Private Interior (reconstruction) category"
Interior Of The Year 2020 Czech Republic - Finalist "Journalists' award"

formafatal

residential

Complete reconstruction of a terraced house in a lucrative part of Prague for a successful Czech film director and his family took four years. The two-story house is surrounded by nature and from the road is accessible only by an external staircase with 80 steps. From the terrace of the upper floor, it offers an incredible view of Prague. In connection with the ground floor, there is a romantic, picturesque garden.

The client desired ostentatious, unusual, colorful living, referring to the book The chamber of Curiosity by Gestalten publishing. The book inspired him in the interiors, approaches, and overall colorful, daring, eclectic solution. The client's wish was to use the upper terrace, where he wanted to build a winter garden to enlarge the interior part to connect it to the exterior and connect the garden with the interior. The whole family is used to live on a houseboat, which is the basis for the perception of space and the requirement of connection.

During the reconstruction, we tried to respond to the client's requirements; we welcomed his openness, courage in terms of color, and non-traditional contrasts and combinations of materials, which combine sophisticated and noble (expensive) materials with the most common cheap simple variants.

Overall, the project was complex. Find a clean architectural solution combined with the disposition of the house and the requirements of the client. Thanks to the various materials and equipment used, the non-traditional solution managed to keep all the contradictory ideas harmonious. The client bought the equipment, furniture, and pendant lamps in various bazaars and antics himself and then in collaboration with the academic painter Miroslav Bednář, who helped him furnish the apartment.

He owns a vast number of books and a collection of paintings, which he wanted to place on almost every wall in the house. He knew from the beginning that he wished to have blue walls where the paintings would stand out nicely. We used a combination of luxury materials - such as red and yellow travertine - in contrast to cheap materials.

award-winning architectural studio

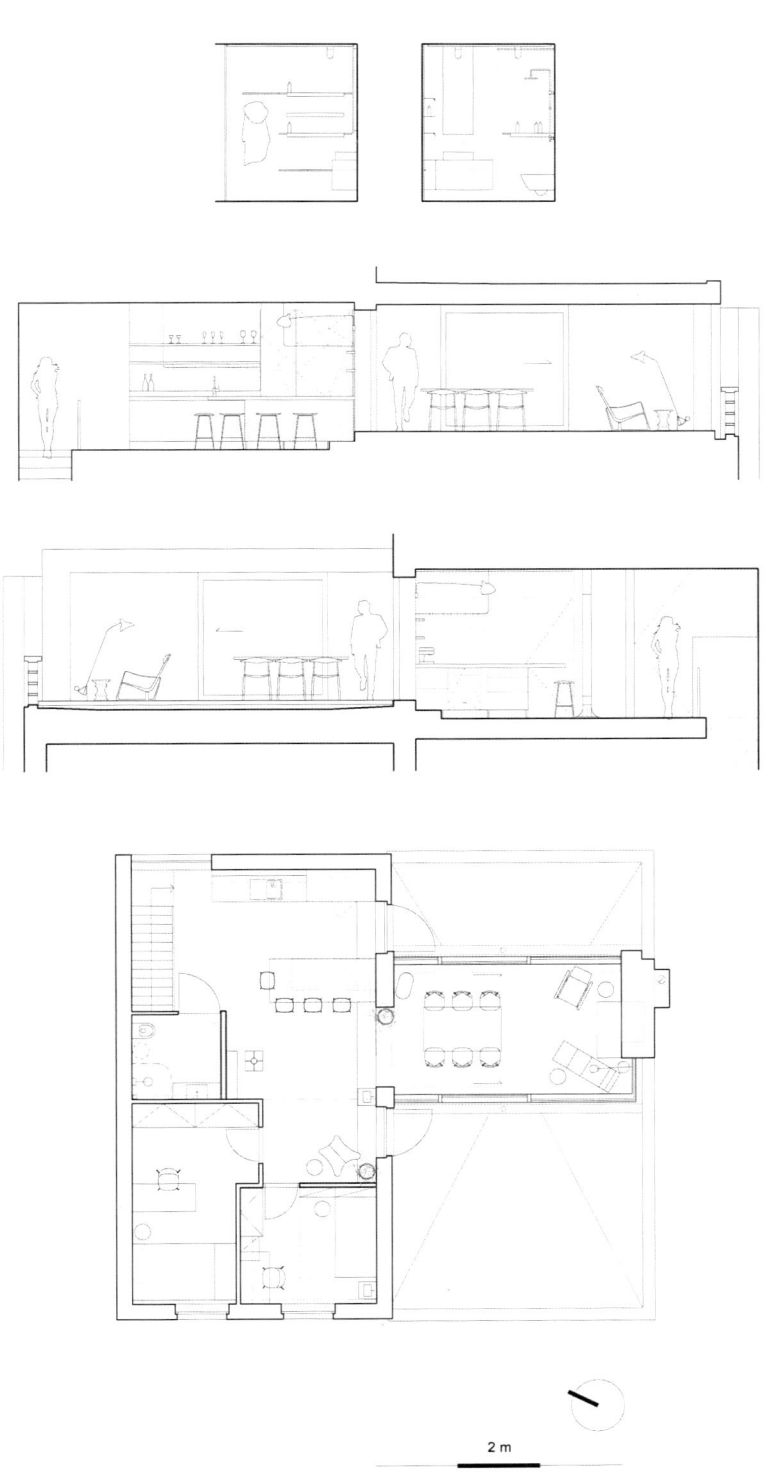

hřebejkovi

residential

award-winning architectural studio

hřebejkovi

award-winning architectural studio

slezská
private apartment

Architect in Charge
Eng. Arch Dagmar Štěpánová
Eng. Arch Dana Szabó

Team authors - architects
Eng. Arch Dagmar Štěpánová
Eng. Arch Dana Szabó

Location
Prague, Czech Republic

Area
Usable floor interior area 142 m^2

Project Year
2018 - 2019

Realization completed
2020

Photo credit
BoysPlayNice (www.boysplaynice.com)

award-winning architectural studio

slezská

The project is a large flat in an apartment building from the first half of the 20th century in the center of Prague. The apartment is for a young family with two small children. The clients did not want to change the apartment's layout, but the rest was a complete reconstruction, including all surfaces.

Given that the owner is a successful manager who travels a lot around the world and feels good in hotels, his idea was based on the comfort of hotels and their style - a five-star standard, surrounded by luxury. The wife, who studied in London, was very inclined to an elegant English style. Nevertheless, they both love art, colors, and an eclectic mood— aesthetics, neatness, comfort, elegance, classic traditional style.

The owners emphasized comfort and the highest quality of surfaces and materials used. Therefore, we aimed to combine three basic principles of the assignment - comfort, which comes from the hotel; elegant aesthetics based on London; colors and eclecticism at the client's request.

The colors of the furniture are related to the paintings that the clients wanted to incorporate into the apartment.

We deliberately contrast styles and combine them to gain glance and originality. All with an emphasis on practicality and comfort.

By breaking through the wall, we decided to create a larger space between the main living room and the library, which also serves as the owner's office, and at the same time, we wanted to fit in the wooden door trim a data projector screen.
We insisted on breaking through the wall because of the visual connection - but it was very demanding in terms of statics.

The whole realization was intended as a combination of styles and materials. Velvet in variety with a modern, timeless shape of the chair. Onyx in the bathroom combined with cement tiles and unique prints on the mirrors, marble in the kitchen combined with a concrete screed.

The bathroom has mirrors with special nanotechnology prints, transitioning from matte to clear, gradient fog. The living area dominates modular sofa TOGO by Ligne Roset from corduroy. The floors are cement tiles, and in areas where there were wooden floors, we sanded and refurbished them. In the whole flat, you can find a combination of custom-made and ordinary furniture.

award-winning architectural studio

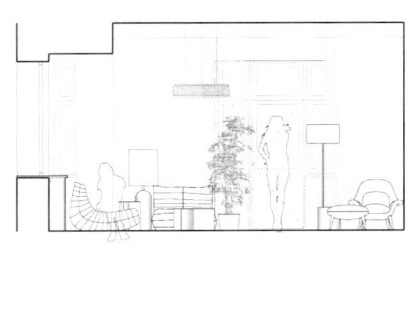
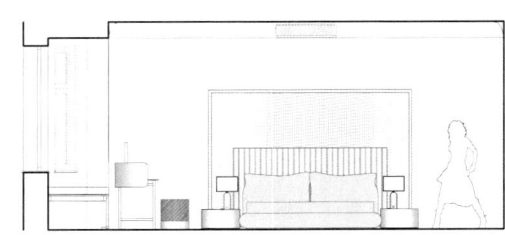
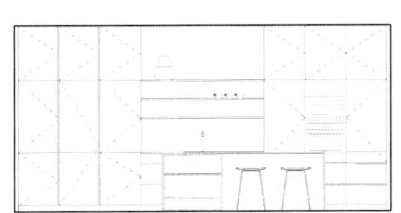
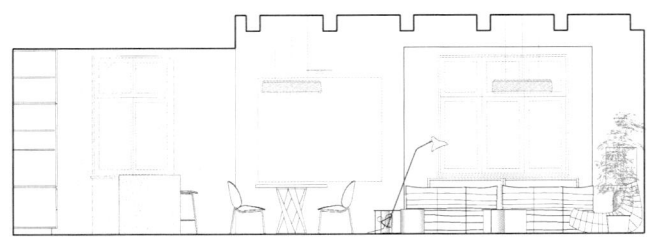

slezská

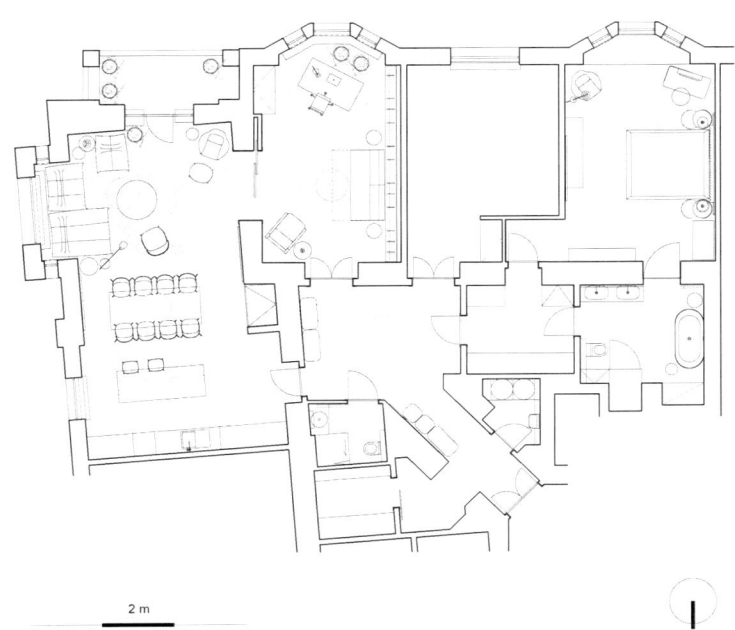

award-winning architectural studio

slezská

award-winning architectural studio

loft hřebenky
private apartment

Architect in Charge
Eng. Arch Dagmar Štěpánová

Team authors - architects
Eng. Arch Dagmar Štěpánová

Location
Prague

Area
Usable floor area 85 m²
Terrace 50 m²

Project Year
2015

Realization completed
2016

Photo credit
BoysPlayNice (www.boysplaynice.com)

Awards & Nominations
Interior Of The Year 2016 Czech Republic - Absolute Winner "all categories"
Interior Of The Year 2016 Czech Republic - Winner "Private Interior (new building) category"
Modern Decoration International Media Award 2016 - Absolute Winner "all categories"
Dolcevita 2016 - Interior Of The Year

This modern flat with industrial taste in a brand-new penthouse on the highest floor is located on a green hill near the center of Prague. It supplements a 50m² large terrace with a lovely view of the luxurious residential area. The lift goes directly to the flat. We deal with a complicated layout thanks to atypically solved pieces of furniture. The total number of us designed pieces ended in figure 44. We added a few iconic pieces of furniture, predominantly created in the '50s.

The owner had only two desires: he asked for one hanging wall, which we had previously designed for the project of a small showroom by Lucie Taschen from reinforcing steel bars. Then he wanted an industrial touch, industrial elements, and materials. Our styles matched perfectly, so he gave us a free hand to do what we wanted; the only limitation was the budget. So we redesigned the apartmentfrom scratch.

We moved the partition walls, removed the doors, took down the white pasting, and tore down the ceilings. We transformed the dull, standardized apartment into a sophisticated man´s residence with an industrial loft-style allure. We removed hard gypsum plaster even on the ceiling and in part of the apartment, thus exposing the concrete parts of the structure to the naked. We followed up on the wishes of industrial elements. By giving us absolute freedom, we tried to repel the owner's personality through his interests.

Due to the complicated disposition of the apartment, we had to use every centimeter square. As a result, there were missing basic things like a technical room and, on the other hand disproportionately large terrace. Atypical furniture has made up many of the shortcomings of space and does not seem strange. Everything is thought up into tiny detail.

The choice of materials was particularly decisive: we covered the walls and ceilings with prefab concrete plates. The floor is covered with industrial cement, and the kitchen and the built-in cupboards have an excellent appearance thanks to the black-stained multiplex. The steel sliding door also conveys industrial inspiration.

What makes the apartment unique is the furniture. We designed 44 custom pieces for the apartment. Here too, the industrial style is apparent, such as the coat hooks made from reinforcement steel-These metal rods were also used in the bed headboard.

award-winning architectural studio

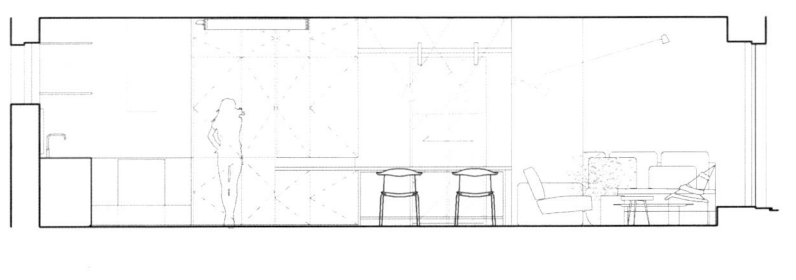

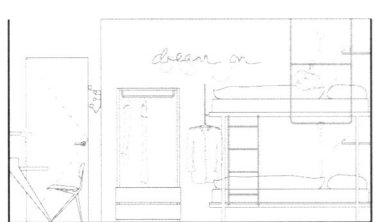

loft hřebenky

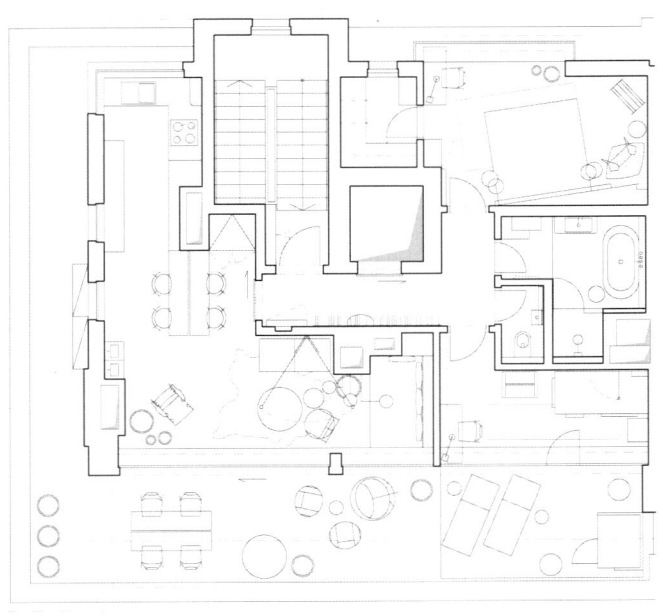

award-winning architectural studio

loft hřebenky

award-winning architectural studio

loft hřebenky

award-winning architectural studio

loft hřebenky

award-winning architectural studio

strom flat
private apartment

Architect in Charge
Eng. Arch Katarína Varsová

Team authors - architects
Eng. Arch Katarína Varsová

Location
Prague, Czech Republic

Area
Usable floor area 94,6 m²

Project Year
2017

Realization completed
2017

Photo credit
BoysPlayNice (www.boysplaynice.com)

The young couple approached us for advice while choosing their future new home. Finally, the choice fell on a spacious, more than 90 m² large apartment, which required a complete reconstruction. The apartment is located in a functionalist house in the center of Prague, but also in the immediate vicinity of greenery.

The client's wish was to create a home that would provide a feeling of airiness and spaciousness. At the same time, they desired to separate the daily activities, so the members of the household will not disturb each other.

By adjusting the layout, we obtained an ample longitudinally illuminated living space. Thanks to the large windows, in connection with the layout improvement, it is possible to see the green treetops even from the central living part of the apartment. We played with see-through views both to the exterior and between the interior spaces of the apartment.

The kitchen with a solid oak dining table at the center of the space, separating the living room and office room, was later converted into a children's room. The bedroom is located in a separate block, interconnected to a day-lit bathroom.

We searched for the central interconnection motif of the interior together with the client, and none of the thoughts was exactly what we desired until we accidentally revealed a beautifully crafted concrete girder ceiling structure, partly with a visible drawing of a wooden formwork.

The new interior was created taking into account the existing elements of the apartment - concrete girder ceiling, massive long windowsills made of black terrazzo, renovated oak parquet floors. We followed these basic details with simple colors and materials - white, black, metal, concrete surfaces, and oak wood.

The connecting furniture element in the main living space is the extensive and long library, passing through the entire width of the layout. The cables are situated in metal pipes and ceiling profiles; the design of switches and sockets (Berker range 1930) was chosen to remind the classic rotary switches.

The walls of the bathrooms are lined with a matt ceramic mosaic, in delicate tones of cream and dim green, complemented by a rough contrast in concrete washbasins, concrete screed on the floors in combination with black metal frames, faucets, handles, and light fixtures.

award-winning architectural studio

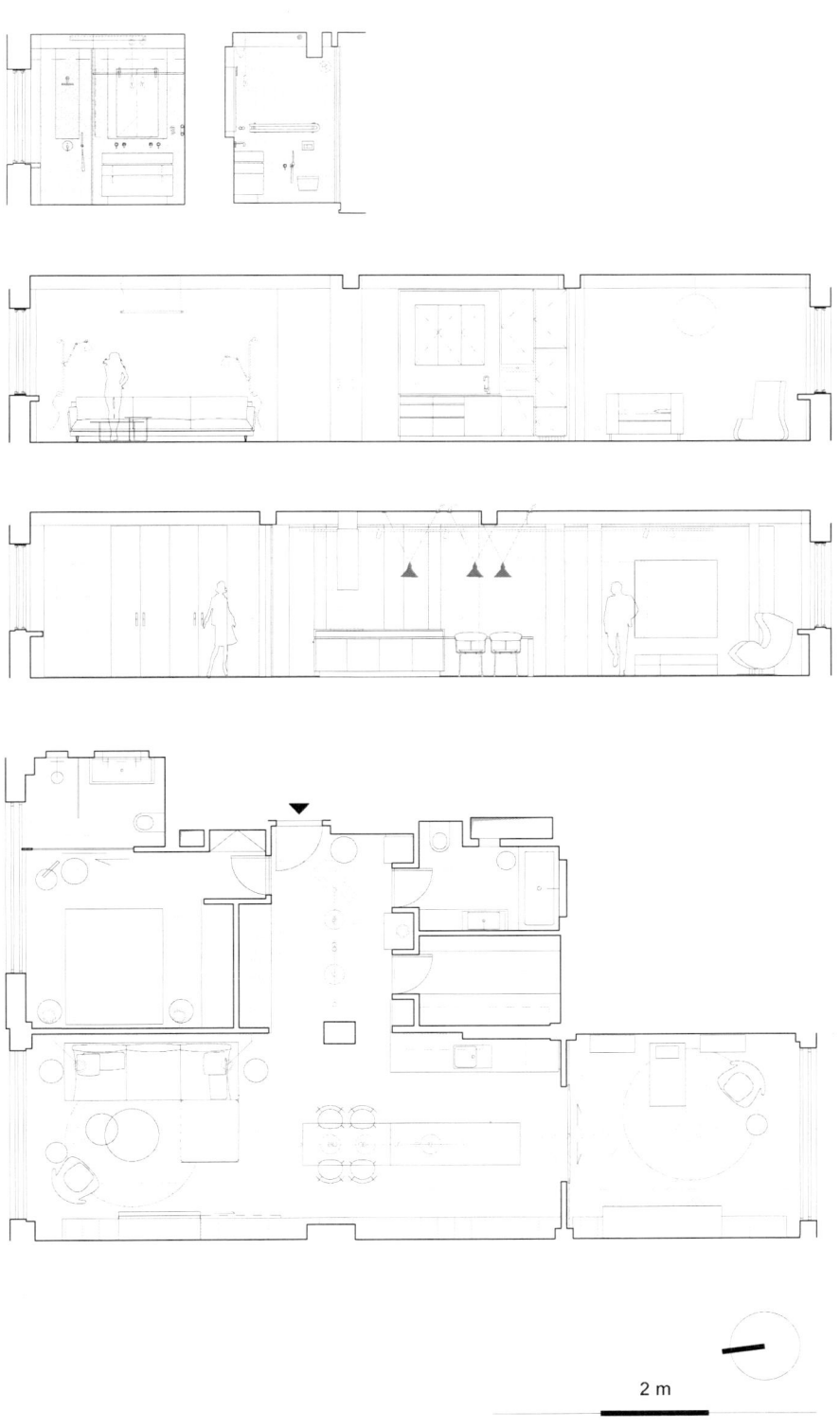

strom flat

2 m

award-winning architectural studio

strom flat

award-winning architectural studio

strom flat

award-winning architectural studio

strom flat

residential

award-winning architectural studio

sri lanka

award-winning architectural studio

happy hills
hotel's apartment

Architect in Charge
Eng. Arch Dagmar Štěpánová
Eng. Jan Roučka

Team authors - architects
Eng. Arch Dagmar Štěpánová
Eng. Arch Martina Homolková
Eng. Jan Roučka

Location
Tangalle, Sri Lanka

Area
Usable floor interior area (standard apartment) 60 m²
Terrace (standard apartment) 35 m²

Project Year
2019

Realization
Postponed

3D renders
David Straka CGI (https://monolot.studio)

Initially, investors approached us to design three types of hotel rooms for the hotel complex. Later, due to the client´s satisfaction, our cooperation extended to the complete interiors of the entire Happy hills hotel, including restaurants, bars, spa, receptions, cafes, etc. We only had the concept design of the main building available when designing rooms. Although together with clients, we interfered in the layout of the hotel, from experience, we saw shortcomings in the architecture, we changed and reshaped the content. The location is on a gentle hill in tropical greenery near the temple, and the place itself offers beautiful ocean views.

In the first phase, the client wanted us to create room designs that resulted in visualizations so that the investors could get more partners to the project. In addition, we wanted to create a modern functional interior with a tropical atmosphere, which reflects the diversity and colors of the island.

We approached each hotel apartment individually and emphasized the variability of the space - sliding panels give the ability to open the area thoroughly and close the room to have privacy. With this variability of changing the room to an open space connected to a terrace, you deny the boundaries with the interior and exterior. For example, the living rooms are located on a covered deck. We can transform the generous open space into separate rooms with privacy and comfort zones thanks to the sliding panels.

The challenge in this project was the joint search for a specific output on an unclear assignment without a particular concept and a precise study of room layouts. In addition, clients were so in the beginning that we felt the need to participate not only in the interior design itself but also in the process associated with the functionality and operation of the hotel. In the interiors, we used concrete, which we left raw, exposed. Muksarabi - partitions that are made of perforated fittings – from fired clay or concrete.

This material is widespread in tropical areas - it let the wind blow out but simultaneously shades, protects from the sun and creates games of light and shadow. This visual divider is a popular principle in interiors in tropical countries. We used different types of textiles, ornamental cement tiles, and natural materials and wanted the interior to be cheerful, playful, and comfortable.

award-winning architectural studio

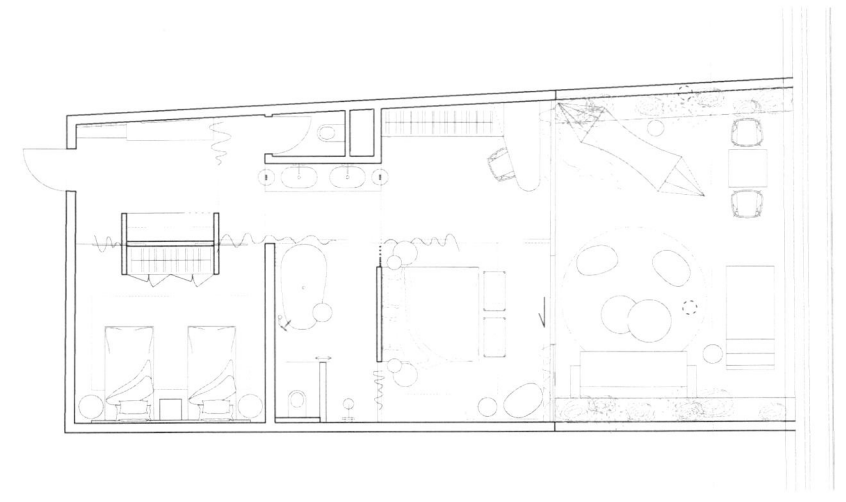

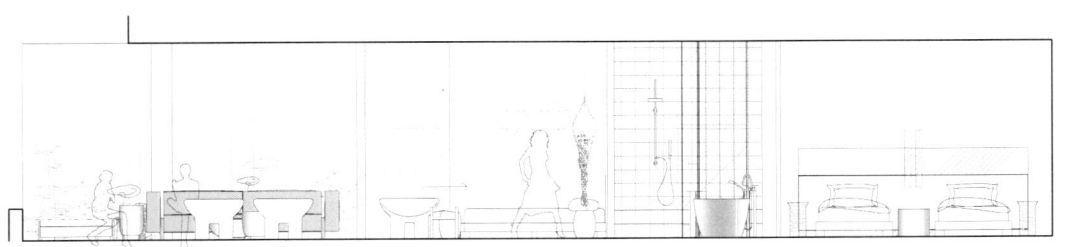

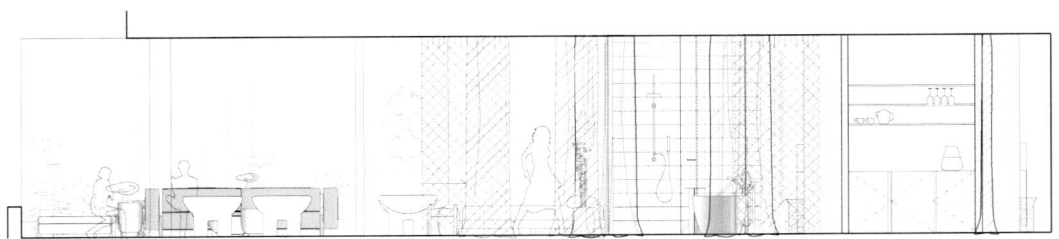

happy hills

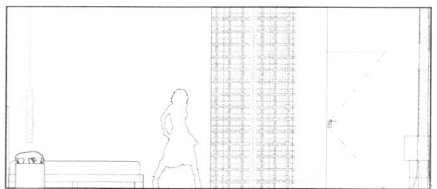 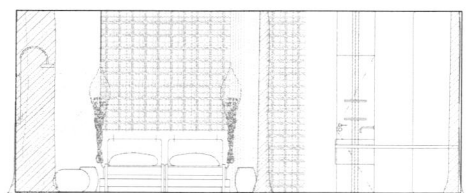

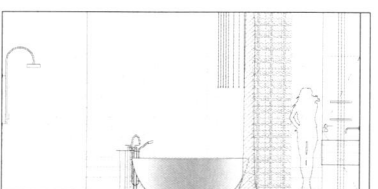 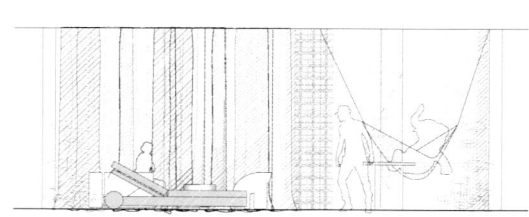

award-winning architectural studio

happy hills

hospitality

award-winning architectural studio

czech republic

award-winning architectural studio

moon club
music nightclub

Architect in Charge
Eng. Arch Katarína Varsová (Formafatal)
Eng. Arch Radek Teichman (Machar&Teichman architects)
Eng. Arch Pavel Machar (Machar&Teichman architects)

Team authors - architects
Eng. Arch Katarína Varsová (Formafatal)
Eng. Arch Dagmar Štěpánová (Formafatal)
Eng. Arch Radek Teichman (Machar&Teichman architects)
Eng. Arch Pavel Machar (Machar&Teichman architects)

Location
Prague

Area
Usable floor area 740 m²

Project Year
2017 - 2018

Realization completed
2019

Photo credit
BoysPlayNice (www.boysplaynice.com)

AWARDS, NOMINATIONS
Surface Travel Awards 2019 - Winner "Bar category"
Big See 2019 - Winner "Hospitality category"
Interior Of The Year 2019 Czech Republic - Finalist "Public Interior I. category)

formafatal

hospitality

MOON
CLUB

Formafatal and Machar & Teichman formed a creative union to design the mysterious Moon club, located in vivid, vibrant Prague city center. The newly opened club brings the brand-new original view on interior design in this city area.

Clients have had the vision to create an interior with details, which would be significantly higher than other enterprises in the surrounding area.

We created the different zones to overlap the original house layout and needs of the club operation. Cozy seating areas with comfortable lounge furniture and mild light intensity are placed under the arch ceiling alongside the central hall, while the dance floor is opposite. One can overview what is happening around the main central bar from the courtyard gallery, move into one of the lounges, or even enjoy the atmosphere in the Alchemist bar located on the second floor.

The club's space, which used to serve for bank administration, connects the central hall with glass roofing. This element of the inner yard was one of the challenges of space solutions and the technical aspect of acoustic, on which we paid great attention. As a result, acoustic measures, such as doubled roof glazing, acoustic buffer wall constructions, and special plasters are incorporated into the interior concept.

The name of the club is linked to the main motive – the Moon. Major topics are the mysteriousness of night-fall and alchemistic mystique. The walls of the 740m^2 club are covered with patina painting, which makes the common link to all the spaces with variations of atmospheres and details. Materials used for interior elements vary through the rooms – patinated metal sheets, dark burned wood, old stained mirrors, ornament paintings on the walls, and velvet upholstery furniture in several elegant colors. Essential is the light atmosphere with diverse intensities, hidden light sources, and design lights and elements.

The central main bar is the dominant unit, with a moon silhouette floating above the yard. Three big round pendant lights and groups of metal pendants above it reflect the glass ceiling. This effect evokes a starry night and creates a deep and magical feeling. The main bar is made with goldish corrugated metal cladding. Finally, there is the floor made from wooden cubes as a reminder of the historical passage function.

award-winning architectural studio

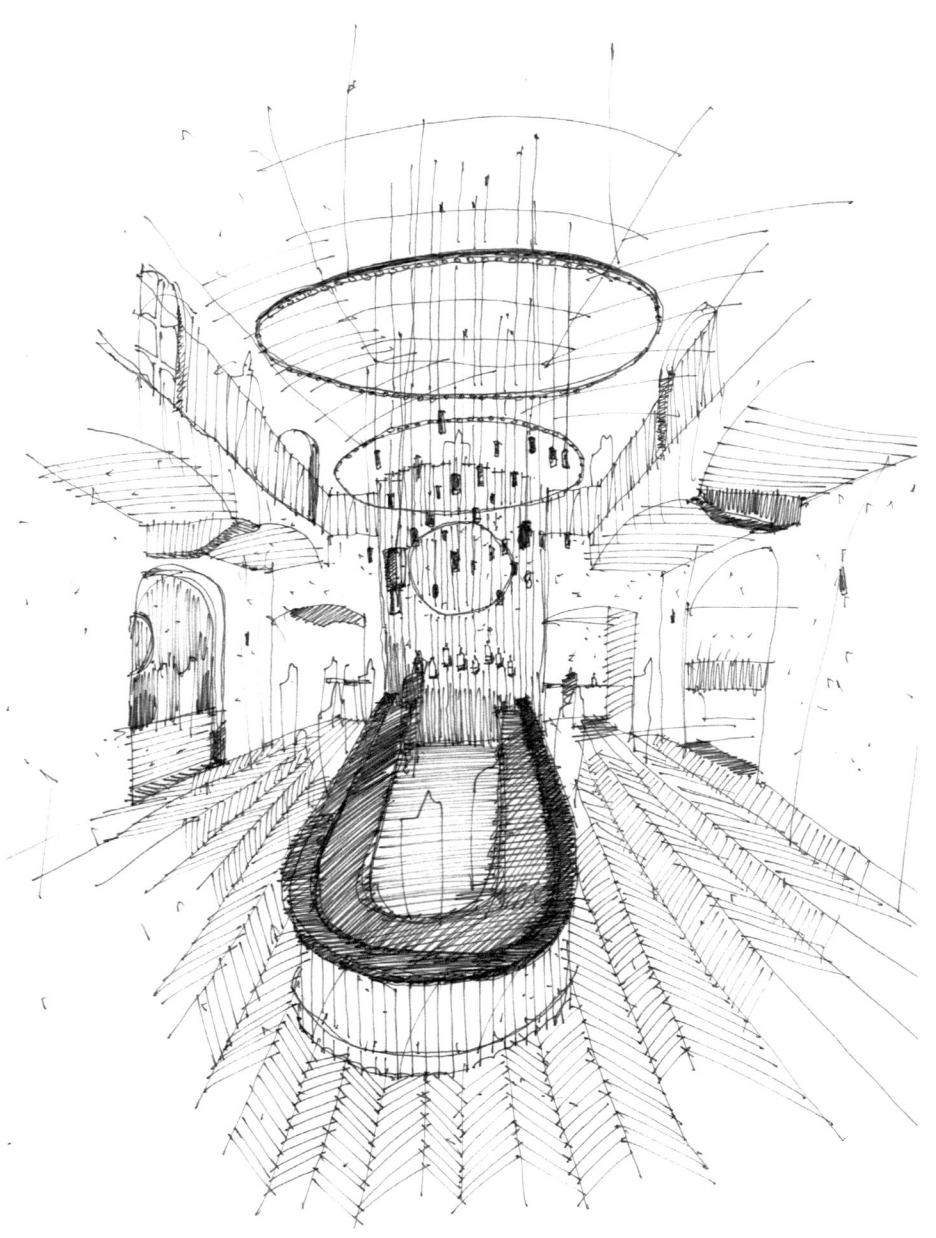

moon club

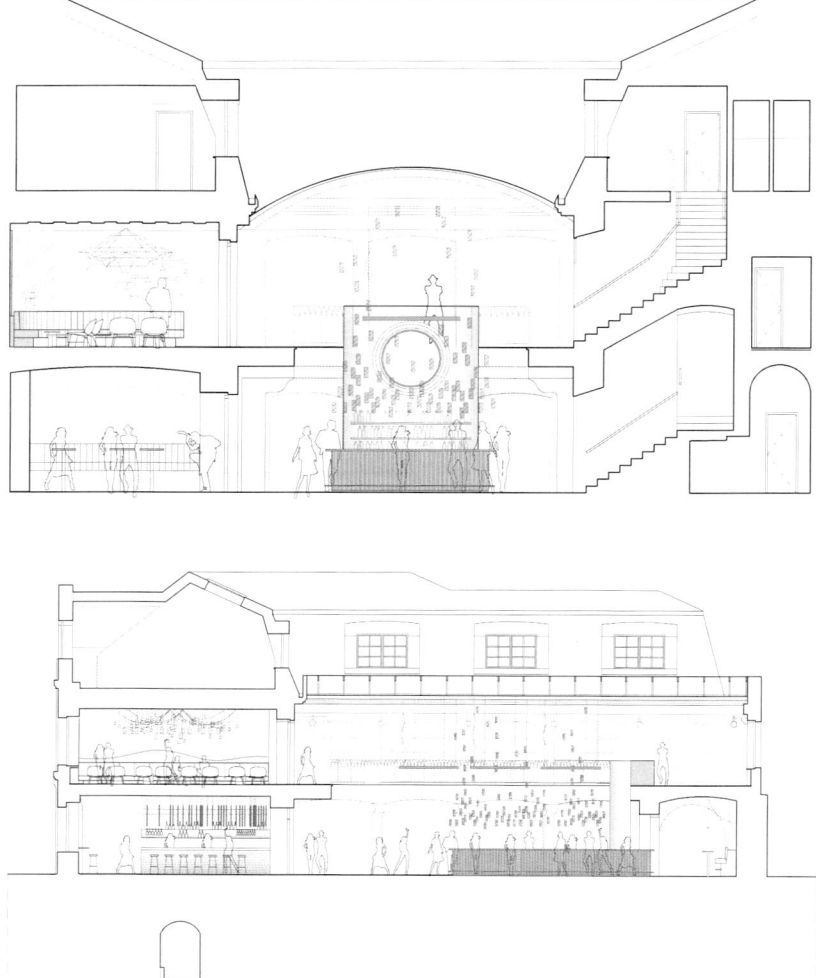

award-winning architectural studio

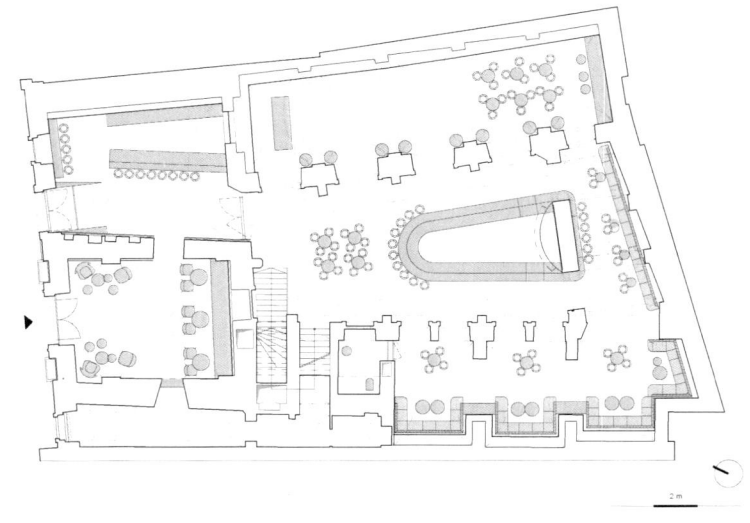

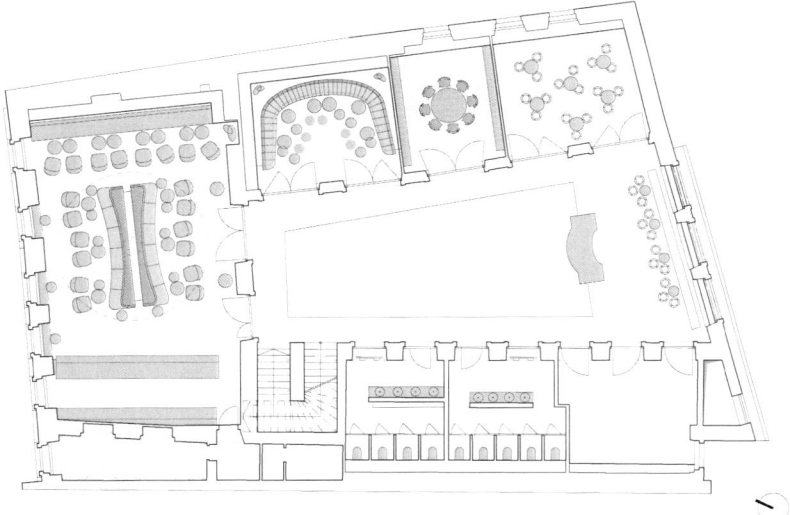

moon club

award-winning architectural studio

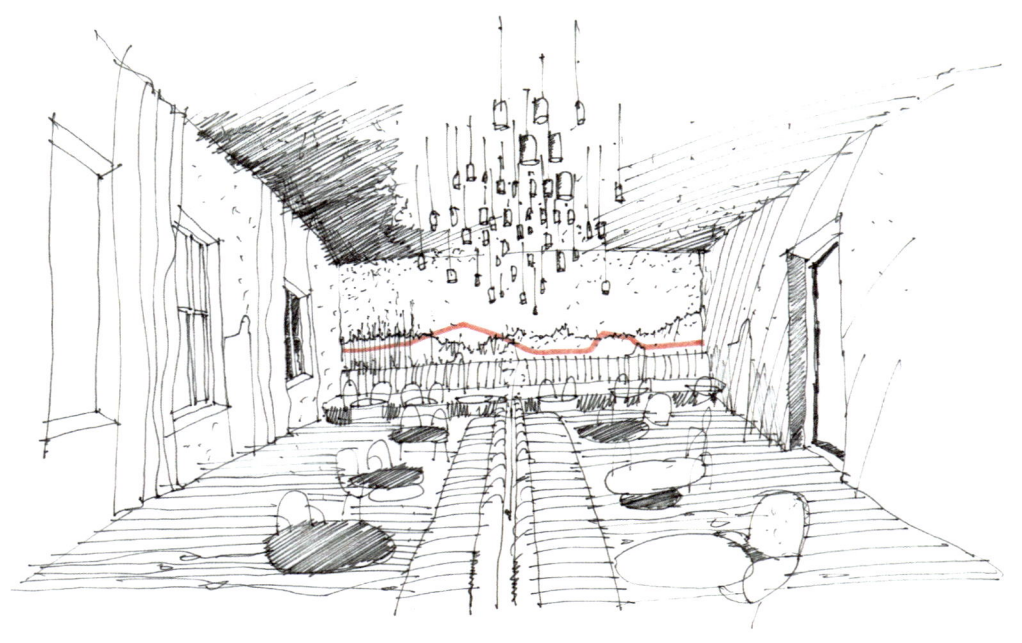

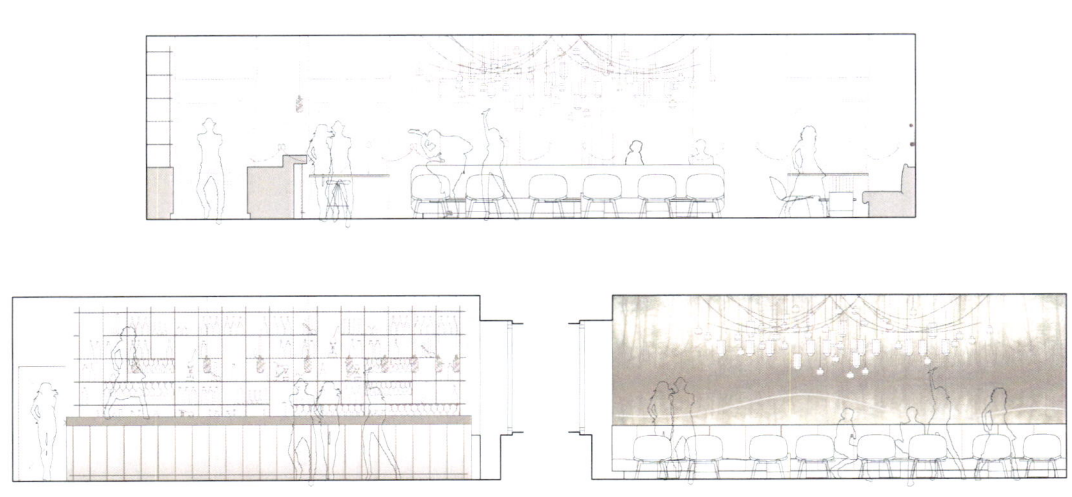

moon club

163

award-winning architectural studio

moon club

award-winning architectural studio

moon club

167

award-winning architectural studio

moon club

award-winning architectural studio

moon club

award-winning architectural studio

gran fierro II
argentinian restaurant

Architect in Charge
Eng. Arch Dagmar Štěpánová
Eng. Arch Iveta Tesařová

Team authors - architects
Eng. Arch Dagmar Štěpánová
Eng. Arch Iveta Tesařová

Location
Prague, Czech Republic

Area
Usable floor interior area 314 m²
Terraces 75 m²

Project Year
2019 - 2020

Realization completed
2020

Photo credit
BoysPlayNice (www.boysplaynice.com)

Awards & Nominations
Restaurant & Bar Design Awards - Shortlisted "Europe - Surface Interiors category"

award-winning architectural studio

gran fierro II

Gran Fierro is an Argentinian restaurant in the center of Prague. The owner is Argentine, originally from Buenos Aires, Juan Cruz Pacin. The restaurant's concept follows the original Gran Fierro I, which the owner was forced to move.

The main task was to use as many elements as possible of the original Gran Fierro I. With the new restaurant, the owner came up with the idea of transformation – to perceive everything more ecologically to the point that he started producing his coal, which he then uses in his grills. Following the Argentine tradition, the kitchen is based on fire. On this basis, we created a new concept, which we implemented in the interior.

We took coal as a part of the interior. As such, we raised it to the motive of the whole restaurant; coal is applied within the interior in several installations. For example, the individual carbons are placed in the concrete blocks of the long wall of the restaurant, creating a symbolic wall referring to the transformation of the concept. Carbon in this presentation acts more like a jewel. In one of the lounges, an entire vaulted ceiling is created from suspended coals.

An unconventional challenge was to use the original furniture in the new space and connect it with new interior elements. This was a clear limit, and it set the direction from the beginning. On the other hand, Gran Fierro I was already so well-known and popular, so it was convenient that the original elements connected the old with the new, the clients still feel like in their favorite restaurant. Due to the limited budget, many materials primarily intended for construction were used for interior works - concrete reinforcements, steel beams, and concrete blocks. The building material was lifted into an aesthetic element. What is usually hidden in the wall here is confessed, uncovered, raw.

The colors are based on Argentine colors. We reattached the backrests with typical Argentinian trouser straps. The whole concept is industrial, used wood, leather, cement screed, concrete. We deliberately chose a very blue floor - acid stain floor. Except for chairs and lamps, everything is custom-made according to FormaFatal design. The serving table for waiters is in the shape of cows; because Gran Fierro was specialized in Argentine beef, the tables are styled like a cow's torso. The cows' heads are also on the toilets.

award-winning architectural studio

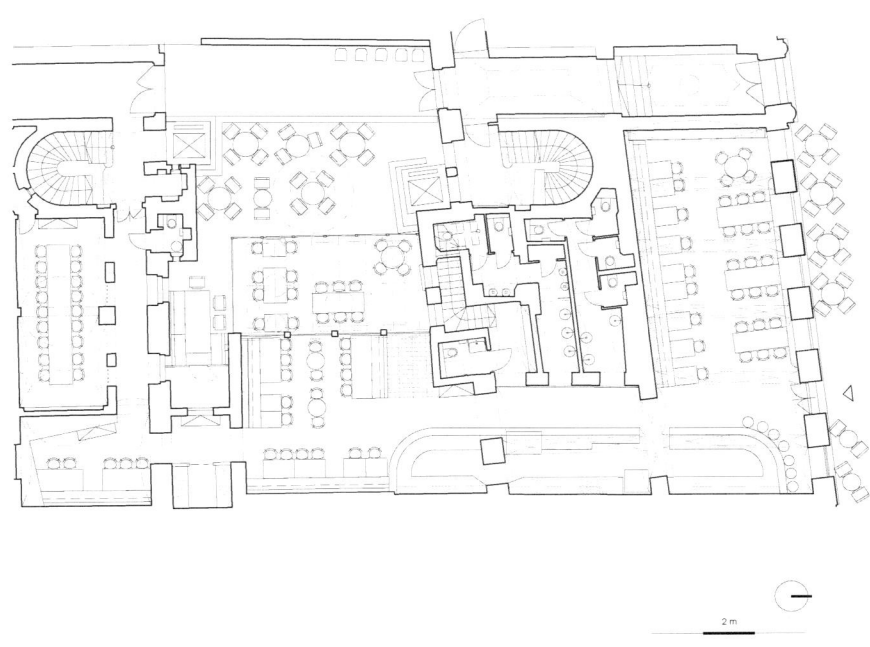

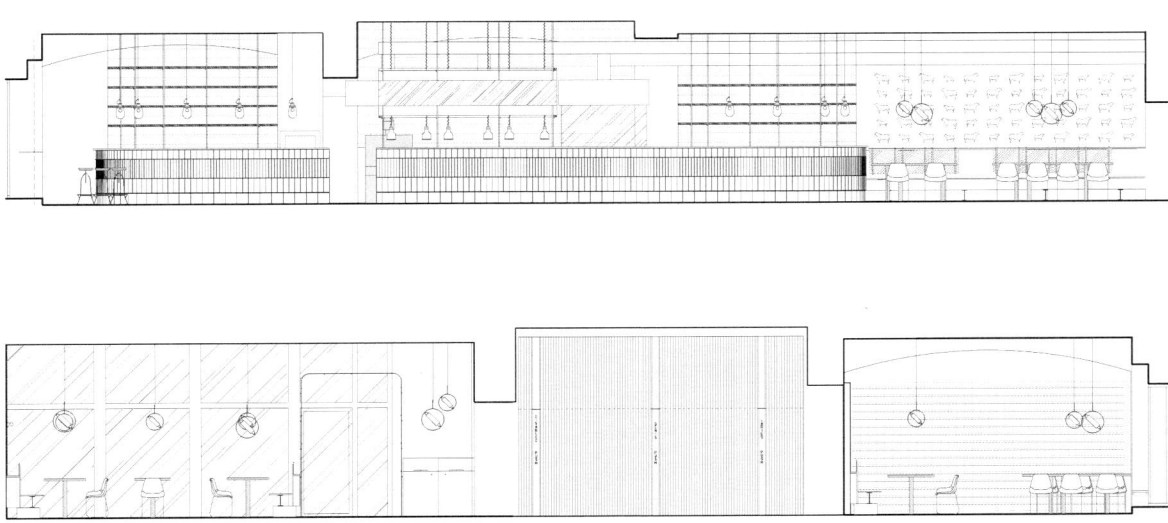

gran fierro II

181

award-winning architectural studio

gran fierro II

award-winning architectural studio

gran fierro II

award-winning architectural studio

gran fierro II

191

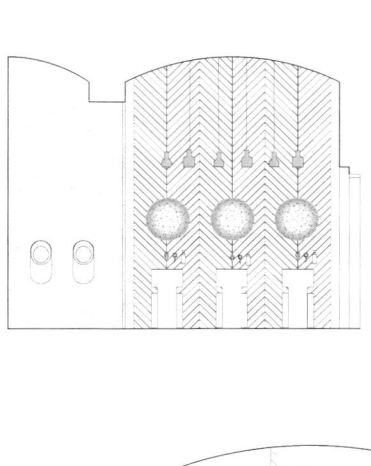

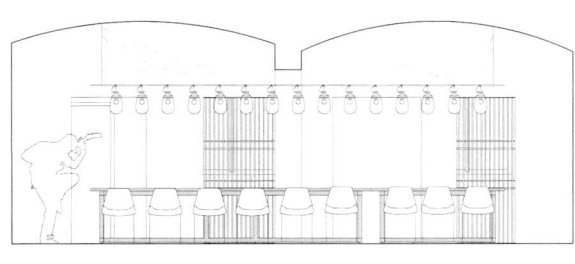
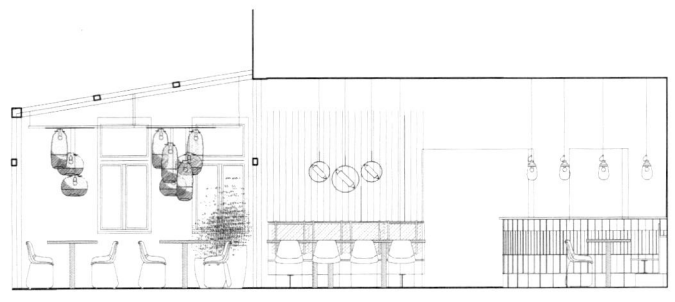
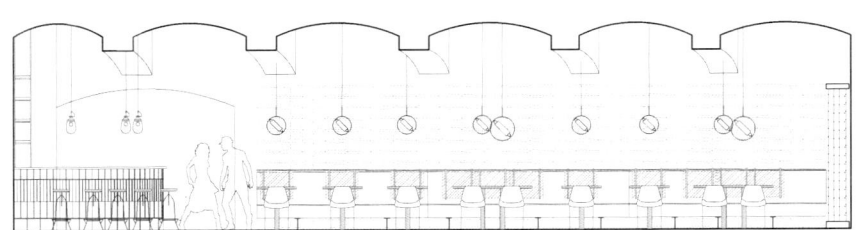

award-winning architectural studio

gran fierro II

award-winning architectural studio

gran fierro I
argentinian restaurant

Architect in Charge
Eng. Arch Dagmar Štěpánová
Eng. Arch Katarína Varsová

Team authors - architects
Eng. Arch Dagmar Štěpánová
Eng. Arch Katarína Varsová

Location
Prague, Czech Republic

Area
Usable floor area 250 m^2

Project Year
2014

Realization completed
2014

Photo credit
BoysPlayNice (www.boysplaynice.com)

AWARDS, NOMINATIONS
Interior Of The Year 2015 Czech republic - Finalist "Public Interior category"

A new Argentinean restaurant was opened in mid-December 2014 in the center of Prague - Gran Fierro situated in functionalistic travertine paneled building in Vorsilska street.

The restaurant owner, Juan Cruz Pacin, is coming from Buenos Aires, and as he has been living in Prague for some time, he decided to bring a piece of Argentina to the heart of Europe. South American cuisine, great cocktails, or evenings with Argentinean tango meet here bar atmosphere where a DJ is present.

We divided the space into two main parts, each at a different elevation. To the well-lighted area at the entrance, dominate a bar in the center, while at the back, you will find a more intimate space with tables, a chill-out zone with armchairs, and a lounge. Still, within the area of 250 m², you can see the kitchen and chefs immediately once you enter the restaurant.

The features are linked up with patina wood tables, shelving systems from metal reinforcing bars, and upholstery made of real Argentinean belts.

The combination of industrial and retro features with South America's touch created space that is definitely worth trying.

Only three months passed from the first appointment with the client to the restaurant's opening; due to the extension of the reconstruction, significant building modifications – including new electrical installation – only two weeks left for the complete concept study and two weeks for a detailed project. I also had to get involved in the realization itself and helped the artisans meet the completion date. In addition, there was a minimal budget for the implementation of the entire interior.

A bar anchors a bright foyer, while in the rear, the space is cozy amid armchairs. Industrial and retro details combine with coherence, warmth, and humor and recall the authenticity of ranch life: pale sky-blue tiles, backlit metal scones in the shape of cattle, wicker pendant lights half-dipped in a gradient of blue, and seating tailor-made from Argentinian belt leather.

award-winning architectural studio

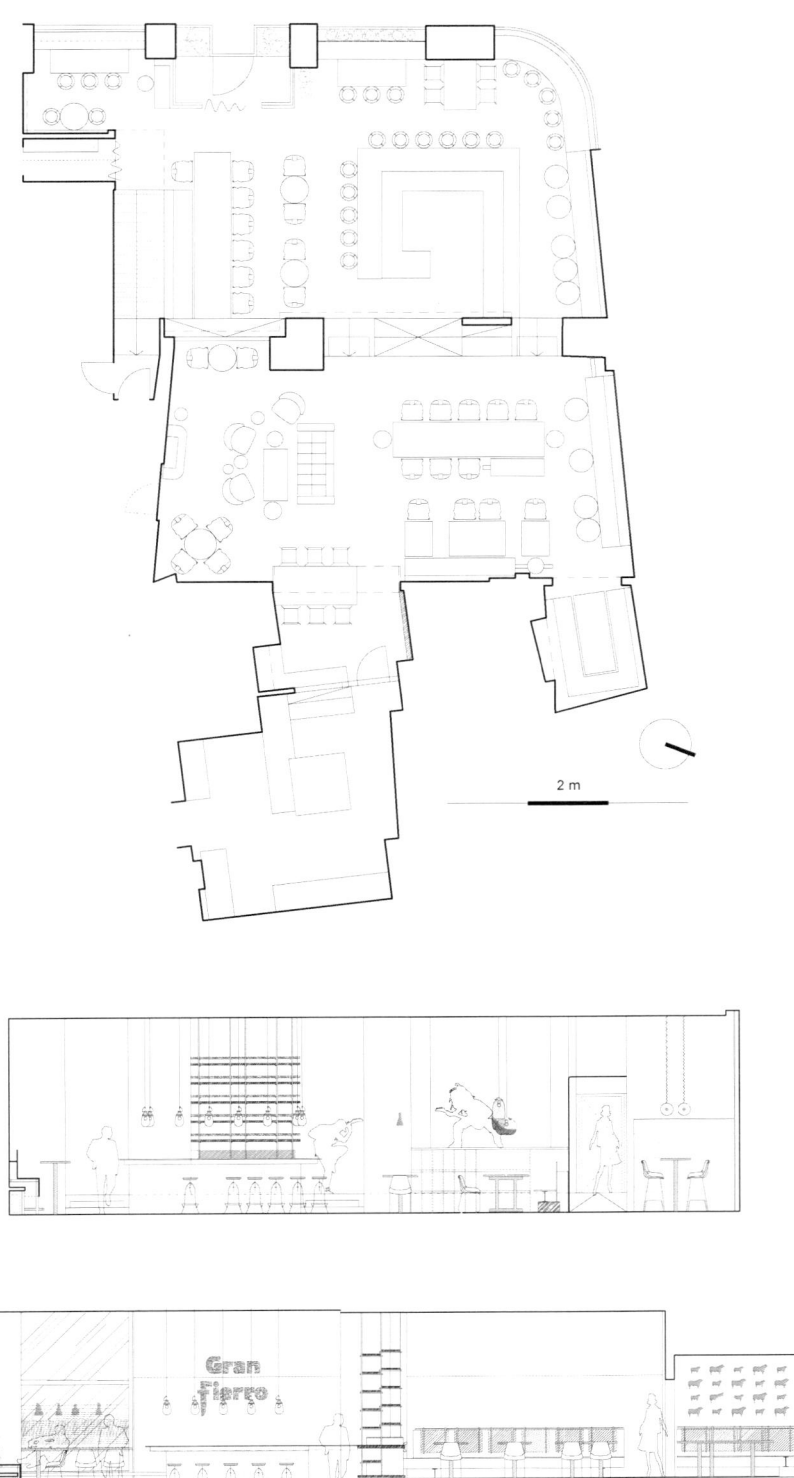

gran fierro I

award-winning architectural studio

gran fierro I

205

award-winning architectural studio

gran fierro I

award-winning architectural studio

autentista
wine and champagne bar

Architect in Charge
Eng. Arch Katarína Varsová
Eng. Jan Roučka

Team authors - architects
Eng. Arch Katarína Varsová
Eng. Jan Roučka
Graphic Designer Janek Dočekal

Location
Prague

Area
Usable floor area 111 m^2

Project Year
2018 - 2019

Realization completed
2019

Photo credit
BoysPlayNice (www.boysplaynice.com)

AWARDS, NOMINATIONS
Interior Of The Year 2019 Czech Republic - Winner "Public Space I category"
Elle Decoration International Design Awards 2020 - Winner "Interior Design category"

formafatal

hospitality

award-winning architectural studio

autentista

Autentista is a wine & champagne bar placed in the historical building (14th century) situated in the very heart of Prague's Old Town. Its name refers to authentic wines and their creators – winemakers, the Authentics who prepare distinctive, natural wines concerning the environment.

The original assignment was to transform an Old Town house's vaulted interior into an inviting and cozy place dedicated to the exquisite taste of natural wines. In other words, to create a space with an atmosphere in harmony with the wines. Authentic wines are a luxury, so the idea was for it to be just as luxurious as the product itself, yet still natural and straightforward.

We wanted to both focus on original architectural elements of the Autentista interior – arched space with a cross vault in the main room – and still create as contemporary an atmosphere and feeling as possible. Therefore, we played with the central axis of the arched rooms, the see-through effect to the backyard window, and placed one of the main features – the wine display – shape is copying the arched room shape. Thus, the wine display becomes the iconic element in Autentista's appearance.

All materials are presented in their original and pure form. The perfect-pigmented coating does not conceal prefabricated steel sections; their natural–

patina—colors shine through. Sanded steel joining elements are left on show, unconcealed. This is what makes those constructions genuinely authentic.

Indirect warm light sources highlight the contours of the vaults and the whole interior with their warm light. Dimmable lights may serve as atmosphere changers, adjusting to different occasions.

Above the bar table, another atypical lamp is made out of a scorched acacia log—acacia wood used to be the go—to material for fence posts marking the vineyards. Its burnt finish increased the wood's soil resistance and, therefore, longevity.

The references to wine and nature can be found in the gradients on the table prints, the cement texture paint on the floors, and the backyard walls. Eye-catching Moooi Meshmatic chandeliers are placed as centerpieces perfectly with the interior concept, thanks to their direct and pure form. Since the investors expressed their wish to incorporate ASCII graphics in the design, the sides of the bar look like a starry night full of constellations consisting only of ASCII characters, created by graphic designer Janek Dočekal.

For the Authentic Wine Bar interior, our studio won the prestigious Elle Decoration International Design Award, category Interior.

autentista

award-winning architectural studio

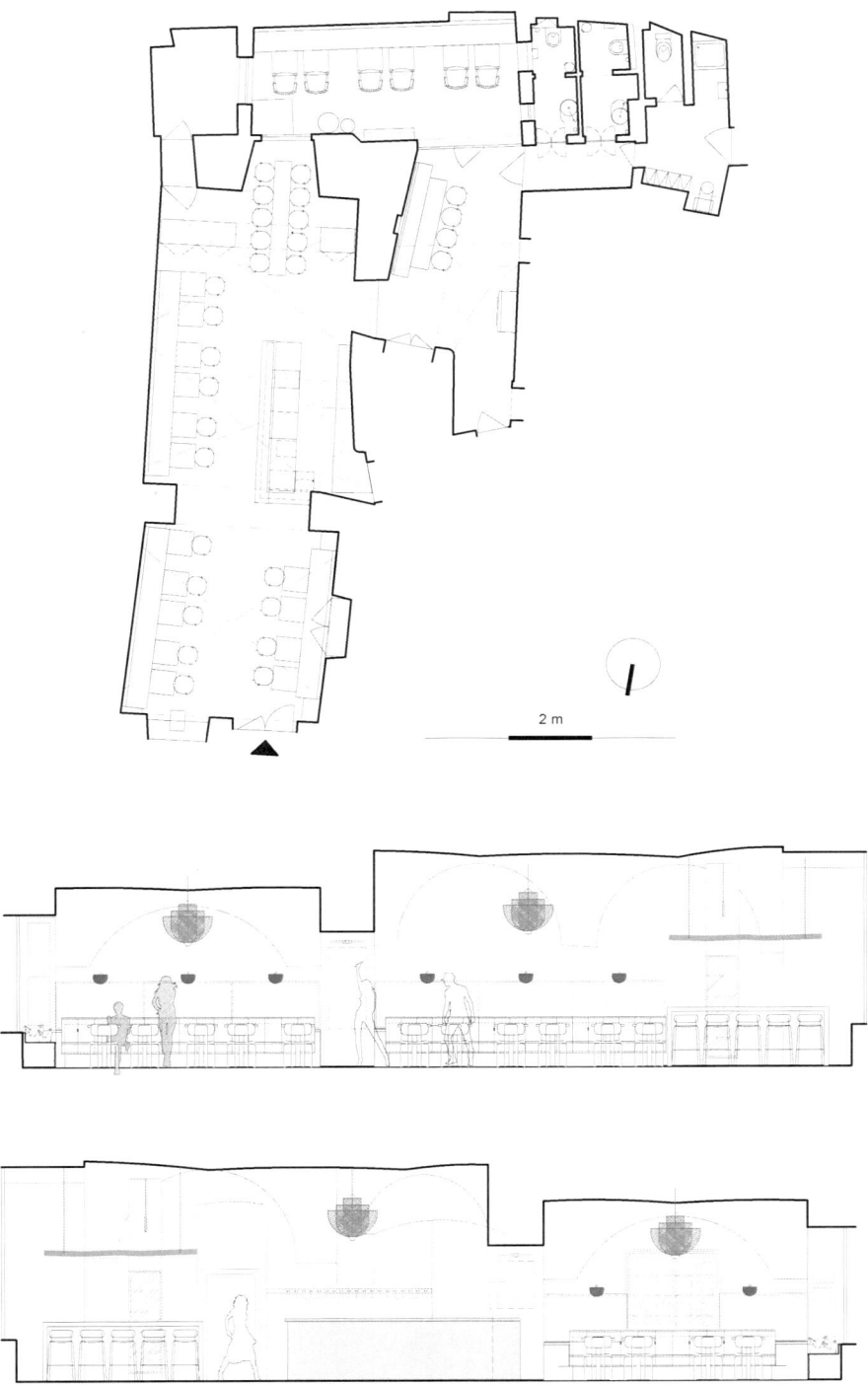

autentista

award-winning architectural studio

autentista

award-winning architectural studio

autentista

award-winning architectural studio

burrito loco
mexican fast food

Architect in Charge
Eng. Arch Dagmar Štěpánová

Team authors - architects
Eng. Arch Dagmar Štěpánová
Eng. Arch Martina Homolková

Location
Prague, Czech Republic

Area
Usable floor area 70 m²

Project Year
2016

Realization completed
2017

Photo credit
BoysPlayNice (www.boysplaynice.com)

AWARDS, NOMINATIONS
Big See 2018 - Winner "Hospitality category"

Burrito Loco is a fast-food network focused on Mexican cuisine with a long tradition in Prague.

The investor has requested studio Formafatal to design an interior for this fast-food chain, the interior marked by strong colors and some stereotyped elements that are easily recognizable by the public. The assignment was to transfer the theme of Mexican cuisine to the interior design, use symbols and features, which would be characteristic for all new establishments that investors will gradually rent.

The interior concept is based on our perception of Mexico – a country full of colors with great variety and glamour in the ceramic tiles, walls, corrugated sheet metal, cladding, and chairs. We have kept the same materials and elements in the design of the individual branches, but we have chosen different color combinations for each of them. The color palette of the cladding of the corrugated sheet metal, the paintings, the ceramic tiles, and the chairs is changing. We have intentionally replaced the characteristic Mexican tiles with monochrome tiles, and we have brought the touch of Mexico through some typical symbols of Mexican pop culture.

We had to deal with a limited budget and, above all, with the atypical assignment, the client wanted to create a whole new interior identity for all new Burrito Loco branches – unification. However, the new/future spaces are diverse (whether in old vaulted houses or functionalist houses) and different sizes. Therefore, we came up with a concept that repeats the core elements and materials (cactuses, sombreros, and corrugated iron for wall coverings). At the same time, the color combinations would be different in each branch.

The essential element is the cactus symbol, dominant in the interior and stylized in different forms. Other features include sombreros and garlands. The hanging lights are made of typical Mexican hats.

The garlands could not be missing at any Mexican party, so they hung on the trees near each tin stand with refreshments. In addition, there are combined garlands of small light bulbs and garlands decorated with a cut pattern in the Burrito Loco interiors. The sombreros as well as the white plastic garlands were ordered directly from Mexico.

The cladding of the corrugated sheet metal symbolizes Mexican residences. The applications on the pillows are in the shape of stylized sun that Burrito Loco has in its logos. Bathrooms are painted with the same flamingo pink of the chairs and the petrol blue of the restaurant walls.

award-winning architectural studio

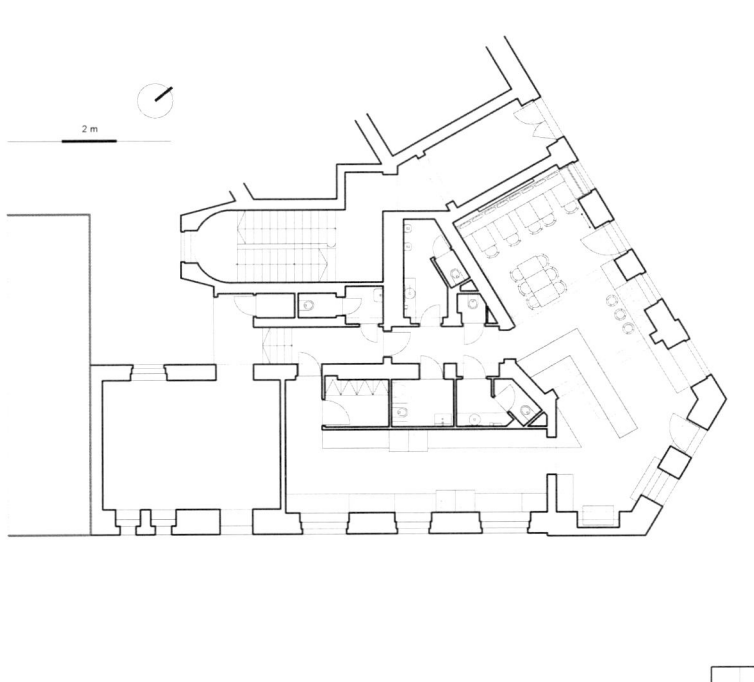
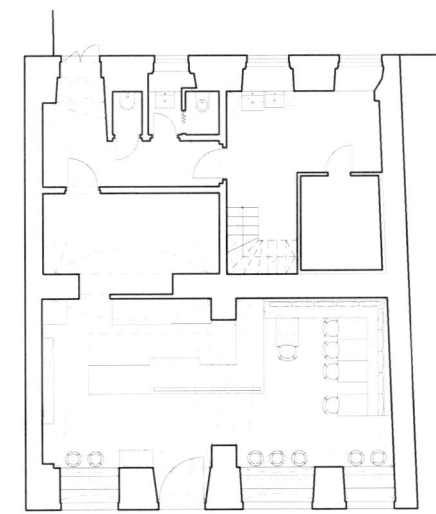
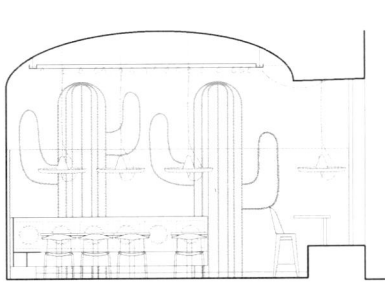
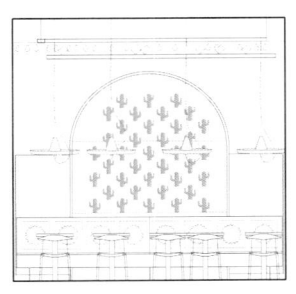
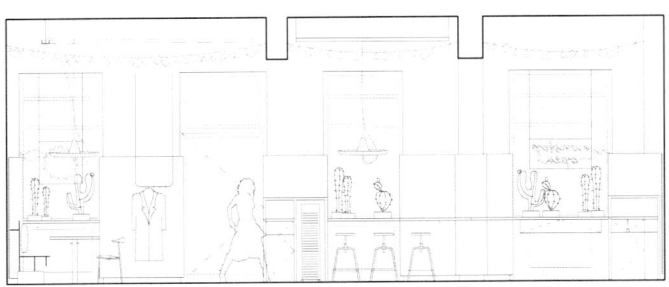
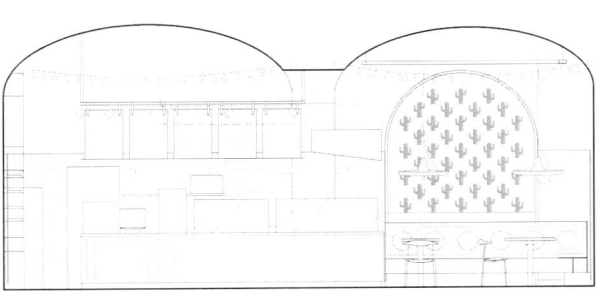

burrito loco

award-winning architectural studio

burrito loco

award-winning architectural studio

burrito loco

www.ingramcontent.com/pod-product-compliance
Lightning Source LLC
Chambersburg PA
CBRC091504220426
43661CB00022B/1310